Mentoring From The Inside Out: Healing Boys Transforming Men

By Reverend Alfonso Wyatt, D. Min.

D1496529

Mentoring From The Inside Out:
Healing Boys Transforming Men

© 2012 By Reverend Alfonso Wyatt, D. Min.
Printed in the United States of America

ISBN 978-0-9859892-2-4

All rights reserved solely by the author. The author
guarantees all contents are original and do not infringe
upon the legal rights of any other person or work. No part
of this book may be reproduced in any form without the
permission of the author.

The views expressed in this book are not necessarily those
of the publisher.

HOLY BIBLE, NEW INTERNATIONAL VERSION®.
Copyright © 1973, 1978, 1984 by International Bible
Society. Used by permission of
Zondervan Publishing House.
Back cover Photography by Jim Belfon
Edited by Rev. Kim Mayner
Cover Photo of William C.J. Wyatt (great nephew)
www.trueperspectivepublishinghouse.com

AUTOGRAPH PAGE

Make it personal by autographing this book to yourself or
as a gift to someone on a quest to mentor others and grow
personally.

Sis Barry...

May these words
be of comfort as you
are called to comfort
others...

Rev Dr. William Wilfand

TABLE OF CONTENTS

ACKNOWLEDGEMENTS

First, I must thank God for giving me the greatest mentor in Jesus. He walked with me through the dark times of my life and continues to teach valuable lessons about love, life and light. I must recognize my mentors in ministry, Dr. Floyd and Dr. Elaine Flake, as well as my spiritual mentor and friend Dr. James Forbes. Closer to home words cannot express my gratitude to my wife, Ouida Wyatt. She saw greatness in me before I saw it in myself and spoke it out loud so that I might hear. I thank thousands of my mentees, in and out of the church, younger and older, that have allowed me space in their lives. Thank you Bro. Shawn Dove; I have lived long enough to be your mentor and now you mentor, guide and care for me as well as so many others. My joy is watching you and all of the brothers and sisters divinely placed in my path become who God destined all of you to be.

I thank my family, first my mother, the Rev. Mae Wyatt, who introduced me to the Lord and gave me the drive to want to be successful through her ever-pressing example and sharecropper's prayers and because you are I am. I want to shout out my siblings, Curtis, Lorraine and Deborah. Thank you for your unconditional love, needed laughs and an always timely lift. I salute caring men and women who guide, protect and love other people's children. I did not write this book with an eye on demographics or fretting over how many units must be moved each month. This book's mission is written to save lives. The last word is for my dear departed father. Daddy, you taught through your consistent and compassionate actions what it meant to be a son, husband, cleric, provider and man. For this I am forever thankful.

PREFACE

I have been blessed to work in the area of youth development for the last four decades. Over much of that time, I served as a mentor, counselor, high school educator, youth program developer, foundation executive, policy advisor, advocate, community organizer, consultant, keynote speaker, national role model and now retired (refired) elder statesman in the field. I am proud to be a mentor and role model to three generations of leaders working in the public/private sectors and faith community concerned about addressing social conditions that impact the lives of young people, families and the broader community.

Parallel to my secular work, I have been a member of the faith community and currently serve as an associate minister on the staff of The Greater Allen A.M.E. Cathedral of New York under the dynamic leadership of Rev. Dr. Floyd H. Flake and Rev. Dr. Elaine M. Flake. I have sought to reach, teach and nurture boys and men through Bible study, innovative workshops, writing, mentoring and preaching. *Mentoring From The Inside Out: Healing Boys Transforming Men,* in retrospect, captures my life's mission to develop boys and men through ministry. This book is not solely about how to be a better mentor. It uses mentoring as a vehicle to first reach the soul of men trying to impact the lives of boys. *Mentoring From The Inside* Out: *Healing Boys Transforming Men* has been supernaturally imparted to lead readers to the door of spiritual transformation. The decision to go through the door (you have free-will) will radically alter how you perceive yourself, others and deepen your relationship with God – all while you grow as a man and mentor.

Spiritual transformation should be the primary goal of one's Christian walk. There will never be lasting spiritual transformation without divine revelation that has the power to expose existential and spiritual truth that were heretofore undecipherable. Revelation is the end process of tearing away the worldly psychological and physical veil that impedes the ability to fully and consistently see, know, love and experience God. Before revelation one *looks* at life and God; after revelation one can *see* a deeper meaning to life and possess a supernatural understanding of God. A spiritually transformed mentor is in touch with self and God. He speaks from a platform of divine insight, not to advance a personal agenda, but to advance the kingdom of God. A transformed mentor has unlimited access to power as a change agent for self, individuals (mentees), families, communities and the church. He is not the source of the power. He is not in charge of the power. He is merely a conduit of the power.

Our young people need and deserve transformed mentors equipped to enter lives caught up in a myriad of societal, personal, peer and family dysfunction. This call to service is for transformed men who can build a sturdy bridge over personal troubled waters while helping young people build bridges over their troubled waters. The process of transformation is not easy and seeking it can be painful. Many erstwhile strong and caring Christians have given up along the way because it is easier to stay stuck than it is to grow. There will be times during the mentoring process when saying, "What's the use the situation is hopeless," or making an equally erroneous decision to superficially read this book. If you find yourself at this crossroad summon the inner strength to press on and not give up. While I did not prescribe "prayer breaks" in the book it should be understood that if you need one you should take one.

The learning architecture of *Mentoring From The Inside Out: Healing Boys Transforming Men* is constructed in this manner: The lead chapter will focus on an issue personally related to the mentor or aspects of mentoring filtered through a youth development and/or societal lens. This is followed by Mentor's Spiritual Reflection consisting of selected men-focused, edited sermons. This is followed by Mentor's Mission Fuel containing: inspiring essays, men focused workshops and retreat findings. Interspersed throughout the book are testimonies from men who mentor or have been mentored.

Every chapter and some essays have a thematic biblical verse that can be used for meditation, discussion and Bible study. Throughout the book are questions to ponder that you may choose to answer at a surface level, or dig deep for answers. For truly bold brothers (men like being bold), these questions can be shared with other mentors creating a much needed avenue for discussion, illumination and male support. Please note that all scripture references are taken from NIV Translation unless otherwise noted. Writings from The Apostle Paul appear in many of the selected preachments because of his uncanny ability to use powerful words and metaphors, usually sports related, to reach men of his time and today.

A special request to women - please understand that this work is focused on men because it is difficult identifying brothers willing to go through the rigors of becoming committed and transformed mentors, mates, fathers or churchmen. It must also be said that women have filled the void on many levels caused by absent fathers, disappearing men, or men who will not or cannot mentor. Brothers who are honest must thank women for their presence, perseverance, love and fervent prayers that have sustained us when we could not sustain ourselves.

Where would we be without praying grandmothers, mothers, wives, girlfriends, aunties and sisters? There are women that have been forced to fill the "man void" caused in part by: spiritual wanting, life circumstances, flawed policies, and plain old bad decisions. While the language of this book is male directed, the gift of personal growth and transformation is not, nor has ever been gender specific. With that said, there is a chapter written by leading sisters who mentor.

In order to set the proper tone for this book, please meet M.B., a 16 year old high school student I met when asked to keynote a "Father to the Fatherless" Conference in Clarksville, Tennessee. When the young brother finished reading his essay there was not a dry eye in the room. The unedited words spoken by this young man should be a clarion call to men.

A father figure is something every child should have - especially males. Growing up with no father figure causes personal problems. Maybe that is why so many teenagers have a lot of issues with our attitudes, emotions, actions and feelings. I was adopted following my birth at Fort Campbell, KY. I never knew my father or mother. My adopted father died in 1994 when I was 4 years old. The last memory I have of him is when he took my brother and I fishing on the Cumberland River. That is my only memory of him.

When my adopted father died, that is when my family broke. My family kicked us to the curb except when they needed something from my mother. My mother did what she could do. She always worked hard and I have respected that. She found ways to spoil us with little things instead of the big things. But I did not have a

father figure. As I was growing up, I taught myself a lot - how to ride a bike, draw, and play games, iron and clean. I think that I tried to make myself believe that I didn't need a father, but there were times when I had questions about fishing, playing basketball, and girls.

I really had no one to look up to. Even when my step-dad came into the picture, that didn't make anything but more problems because we didn't have that father-son bond. He was just there to please my mom. So I looked past home and took to the streets. By my teenage years I didn't trust a lot of people and didn't hang with people my age. My associates were either grown or close to it. I was too mature for my age and so was my attitude. I started smoking, fighting, stealing, and lying. None of that helped me get through life easier - it helped me get locked-down quicker. But I never realized that until after I was 16. That was when I figured out that I was worth something.

I have three little brothers and a sister. I want them to have a male figure to come to and talk to about any situation. Just because I found out the hard way doesn't mean they should have to. When I have children, I want to be a good father. To me that means taking them to the park, taking them fishing, being there for father-child talks, and being there for discipline.

FOREWORD

By Clifford Simmons
Co-Founder Blue Nile Rite of Passage, Inc.

I DARE YOU! Yeah, I said it... I DARE YOU! I dare you to take the wonderfully crafted tools, messages, scriptures and knowledge contained in this book and start mentoring a child or start a mentoring program. I DARE YOU to **not** point the finger at youth but commit yourself to discipline, teach, guide and uplift a young person in your community. Mentoring is needed now more than ever, yet it has always been an integral part of our community... It was called 'The Village'. Somehow, our 'neighborhood' became 'the hood' and we lost our way, yet, it is not rocket science to get it back. It will, however, take men and women to make a serious, committed, focused and unwavering effort to reach one, teach one and save one... I DARE YOU!

Our youth are not the problem; it's a lack of adult supervision, love and guidance. Youth need affection, attention, correction and direction. Without positive adult/parental guidance youth are left to learn about life from the streets, their peers, television or by what they hear in music. They become grown boys and girls never achieving manhood and womanhood. A youth cannot aspire to become something that they have not seen or experienced. Mentors can be the transformative key in helping steer youth in a positive direction, however, true mentors must be consistent, honest and truthful. I challenge you to NOT over commit yourselves. It is better to under commit and be an asset than to over commit and become a liability to the organization you are mentoring for and the mentee that you would ultimately be letting down.

I have been blessed to lead an organization that has helped transform countless lives of youth for the past 19 years called Blue Nile Passage, Inc. (www.bluenilepassage.org). This manhood and womanhood training program was started in 1994 at the Abyssinian Baptist Church in Harlem and incorporated in 1996 and now accepts youth from the NY tri-state area. The main component is a rite-of-passage program for male and female youth and each youth is paired with a one-to-one LIFETIME mentor. Mentor training, meetings, screenings, and reporting are required and mentors must seriously commit to the requirements of the program... no exceptions!

I am reminded of a quote by the mentor of Martin Luther King, Jr., Dr. Benjamin E. Mays, former President of Morehouse College, who said: "The circumference of life cannot be rightly drawn until the center is set". The question is: "What is your center and what is our children's center?" Is it sex, drugs, music, a job, a man/woman, money, etc.??? If it is not God and finding your purpose in life (discovering what gifts/talents you were sent to *give to the world*) then you are probably **OFF** center and your gifts/talents may be buried with you. *I believe the most important thing that a mentor can do is help their mentee find their purpose.*

I applaud my friend and my brother in Christ, Rev. Dr. Alfonso Wyatt, for this wonderful book of wisdom and guidance to those seeking to understand the importance of commitment and responsibility required for any person or organization looking to participate in mentoring. I hope that you not only read it but take time to answer the questions posed at the end of each chapter. My sincere prayer, however, is that you apply the lessons, use them as a guide and pour yourself into the life or lives of youth in your community. This book is even more powerful because it contains the MOST IMPORTANT element that is often lacking in mentoring programs: spirituality or grounding in a higher source... GOD.

Clifford B. Simmons
Executive Director/Co-Founder
Blue Nile Passage, Inc.

CHAPTER ONE

MENTOR'S CALL AND RESPONSE

Then I heard the voice of the Lord saying, "Whom shall I send? And who will go for us?" And I said, "Here am I. Send me!" Isaiah 6:8

When I was called into ministry (getting up off the pew and working for The Lord) I was paralyzed by the agonizing feeling that I was not worthy. My biggest fear of donning a robe was gaining the trust of people (in and out of the church) and somehow disappointing them. I was haunted by my unworthiness. It was as if my brokenness conspired with my doubts to hold me back. I took enough counseling courses to know about conscious, subconscious and unconscious realms that influence behavior. I did not want something leaping out of the depths of my being that would hurt someone 'foolish' enough to believe in me. I was traumatized by the thought I was an unworthy pretender and would be found out.

It was during this time that I began to seriously question the infallibility of God because of the "king-size" mistake of tapping me to preach. I felt content to ignore the call or at least I tried. After several years of running I discovered that God was truly omnipresent. No matter what direction I tried to flee the Lord was right there waiting for me. One would think that I would have grown tired of running. I took many twists, turns, and detours in a vain attempt to lose God. I became more determined to run in what I thought was the opposite direction of where I assumed God would be found. No matter where I went, I was on the path that led to my destiny. I rationalized that I was a good pew member and thought nothing wrong to sit in the congregation, pay tithes and go out and help young people in distress as my secular job dictated. This was a familiar routine that I saw no reason to change.

I felt I benefited from the second chance given to me after being saved. I strongly felt my 12 hour days working in a youth program and sacrifice of my personal life were adequate payback. The question, more like my defense was: What more could I do? I left home in the morning and returned late at night. The answer I could always bank on was that there was no time left in the day to become a minister. A series of mind-blowing events happened that convinced me that God was serious about calling me.

One day while on my way to work, the Lord finally responded to my feelings of unworthiness. Here is what I heard in my Spirit that began yet another level of transformation inside of me: "I know you are not worthy, but I called you and will make you worthy." The scripture: Not by power, not by might but by my Spirit came to mind. It is something to think that you are charged, out of the strength of your personhood, to effect multilevel, multisystem, multidimensional change. This Word freed me of this erroneous assumption and also challenged me in a new way.

Men, you have been called to be a mentor to a young brother in need of spiritual guidance, direction, encouragement, male-bonding and a sense of belonging to something bigger than self. Be very clear, your decision to respond to this call is also a decision to minister to young people informed by the real life struggles you have overcome or still battle, prayerfully with victory in mind. Research shows that mentoring is an effective way to impact the life of a young person. There is wisdom in pairing a teacher with a person in need of their knowledge and guidance. It has been said when the student is ready the teacher will appear. That is why you have to answer this call. Mentors in the faith community, like all other called ministers, must be held to a high standard because they represent the essence of Christ and by extension, the church to the young person, his family, fellow parishioners and the community.

I marvel at people called to ministry who are not concerned or, sadly, unaware of the awesome responsibility or the price they will have to pay. The call to ministry is more than feeling a sense of pride in becoming part of the chosen of the chosen. The call to ministry cannot be seen as the end point in one's "religious" career. Be very clear, with the call to serve, trials and tribulation will surely follow.

It would be enough if you were trouble's main target, but our diabolical adversary never learned how to fight fair. Nothing or no one is out-of-bounds. This is not stated to scare you off from responding to the call to mentor. The reality is that once you say yes it may seem like all hell is about to break loose. The more damaging you potentially can be to the 'ungod's' domain and authority the more hell you will catch.

Peter has a word that speaks to this reality.

> *Beloved, do not think it strange concerning the fiery trial which is to try you as though some strange thing happened to you; but rejoice to the extent that you partake in Christ's sufferings, that when His glory is revealed, you may also be glad with exceeding joy.*
> *1Peter 4:12-13 (NKJV)*

It would be easy to say becoming a mentor should not draw the same ire from the adversary as becoming a pastor, evangelist, deacon or trustee. This 'adultist' view is supported by leaders and pew members alike that do not look at youth ministry as being on par with outreach targeting adults. Our adversary likes this line of reasoning, because young people are and always have been valued targets. The enemy's mission is to stop a young person before he or she can grow to vow "For God I live and for God I will die." It's as difficult to reach the churched and unchurched youth as it is to find men who will answer the mentor's call.

It would be wrong to assume that mentoring is a modern phenomenon created to help troubled teens make life-altering adjustments. Mentors have been called throughout the Bible. The pairing of Elijah and Elisha represents a classic traditional mentoring example of an older more experienced man taking a promising young person under his wing. What should not be lost in this pairing is that, first, this hook-up was ordained by God, and second, Elisha (the mentee) asked for and was granted a double portion of Elijah's (mentor) power. This should tell mentors to interact with their mentees from a Divine assignment perspective and in a manner that encourages their charge to surpass their accomplishments.

It is not helpful for a mentor to work hard to keep their mentee several paces behind. Elijah was able to teach the nuance of being a prophet by having his mentee watch and follow his lead. The elder prophet was clear that it was not only his words that counted but also his behavior. Elijah did not prescribe to the flawed adage, "Do what I say not what I do." This hypocritical philosophy sadly evidenced in faith-based and secular youth programs strips mentoring of its power.

An example of a negative mentoring relationship recorded in the Bible is the tragic mismatch pairing of King Saul and David. Saul was not comfortable grooming his young, dynamic, brave, handsome, athletic, popular and talented protégée. Over time Saul grew suspicious of David as he became insanely jealous of his gifts, talents and promise. He ultimately tried to slay him. Was it the song: Saul has killed his thousands but David has killed ten thousand that drove him over the edge? Or was it the adoring cheers that used to follow him but now followed David that made him bitter? King Saul did not have sincere words of praise, guidance or encouragement for his mentee and ultimately became a destructive force in his life.

Keep in mind Saul knew that David would be his successor and this was a divine mentoring assignment but his flesh still could not handle the burden of grooming his replacement. His base emotion and insecurity took over. What he was called to build up he managed to tear down. If there is no love, no respect, no trust, no rapport there is no possibility of developing a productive mentoring relationship. Saul went from being David's mentor to his tormentor! Scriptures suggest that Saul suffered from low self-esteem. His lack of confidence was in evidence for all to see when at his coronation he was found hiding behind baggage rather than face the crowd gathered in his honor. Was Saul hiding because he was from the smallest Tribe (Benjamin) and felt inadequate to respond to the call to lead or was he trapped by his DNA? It does not matter the cause, especially when the effect was detrimental to his personhood, kingship, country and ultimately his relationship with God.

A view of successful transformational mentoring is how Jesus caught, taught, led and groomed an eclectic, rag-tag group of fishermen, a tax collector, a doubter, a doctor and a dishonest accountant. The Lord always taught by example and never stooped to using fear, intimidation, ridicule, divide and conquer techniques as tools of motivation. Jesus never talked down to the disciples nor constantly reminded them that they were inept 'nobodies' before meeting Him (rampant ego). Jesus spoke the truth, not to be right, but a truth that always led to a higher revealed truth. The Lord used many methods (especially parables) to get His message across through teaching, praying and living out what He preached before the disciples and people.

Jesus always kept the big picture in mind (The Kingdom of God). He did not get lost in irrelevant, trivial, time-wasting arguments (i.e. who will be the greatest in the Kingdom?). Our Savior was anointed to bring out the best because he expected the best even out of flawed flesh (like Peter and Judas). He told his mentees, "Greater works shall you do" as a way of setting high expectations and for the time when they would have to operate without Him. Jesus was the first to use love as a transformative weapon to fight hate. He was focused and mentored with a purpose in mind. While He told the disciples He would make them fishers of men there was something broader and deeper that guided His ministry and mentoring found in Luke 4:18:

> *"The Spirit of the Lord is upon me because he has anointed me to preach good news to the poor. He has sent me to proclaim freedom for the prisoners and recovery of sight*

for the blind, to release the oppressed, to proclaim the year
of the Lord's favor."

Jesus was consistent — even when He became agitated with His mentees. He did not turn His back nor held grudges. He would chide the mentees when necessary asking questions like, "where is your faith or how long will I be with you?" Though frustrated in the natural Jesus never made fun of the disciples or lauded Himself over them. He used frustration and failure as teaching tools to let His mentees know there was a deeper level to their development and purpose.

So my brothers you can learn sound mentoring techniques through secular reading and training, as well as studying mentoring examples found in the Bible. There is an urgent cry in the land for trained, mature, moral, Spirit-centered and Bible literate men armed, focused, prayerful and hopefully dangerous, not to each other, but to the 'ungod's' unholy realm. Our adversary has been described AS a roaring lion but IS not a lion. In the course of responding to your call – when the adversary is on your tracks… please don't get AS and IS mixed up!

Questions to Ponder

1. Do you feel called to be a mentor; if so, what "attack" are you currently experiencing or have you dealt with in the past as a result of responding to your call?

2. Can you give and analyze other biblical mentoring examples like the three offered in this chapter?

3. What key learning (something that you did not know but now glad you now know) did you take away after reading this chapter?

MENTOR'S SPIRITUAL REFLECTION
HELP WANTED

Romans 12: 9-21

Imagine if a job description for men interested in becoming a mentor was written in the Bible. Nestled in Romans 12 is a list of expectations that can be used to set benchmarks for men considering mentoring or for any office in the church. It is important to say that no man will line up perfectly against all of the presented criteria. What this list accomplishes is to show strengths, blind spots and possible areas of growth.

1. **Love must be sincere.** Love should not be manipulative, halfhearted or conditional meaning if I do this for you then you must do that for me. When love is used as a bargaining chip to 'emotionally hustle' a person in order to accumulate things, one person will always feel used and devalued.

2. **Honor one another above yourselves.** If you are going to do God's work you must check your ego at the door. The non-scientific (hear Freudian) definition of ego is when one Eases God Out. When self gets in the way energy and effort that could be directed toward helping a person or changing a situation is ultimately wasted on nonsense.

3. **Bless those who persecute you.** On this count we can all be fired or not hired. It is not easy to turn the other cheek or not seek revenge when wronged. It is no easy task to avoid seeking personal justice in the face of real or perceived injustice.

4. **Be joyful in hope, patient in affliction, faithful in prayer**. When you can't be joyful, patient or faithful that is the time to take a mental health or spiritual health day. No one is 'fit as a fiddle' every day. The vicissitudes of life creates peaks and valleys in our personal life and spiritual walk. Please do not take mentees or other people who depend on you on your life's roller coaster. A good worker strives for balance.

5. **Never be lacking in zeal but keep your spiritual fervor.** Make time to recharge your spiritual batteries. If you give out you must take in. Some workers take pride functioning on fumes. This is not wise. A pilot cannot effectively fly a plane when tired. Likewise, a worker in the vineyard is not effective when exhausted.

6. **Share with God's people who are in need. Practice hospitality.** Men this does not mean donning an apron. It is important to have a demeanor that attracts people in need. It is difficult for a person needing help to approach a person with a 'get away from me' affect.

7. **Do not be overcome with evil but overcome evil with good.** It is imperative to always remember your mission and the source that provides the power to achieve it. Using ministry to settle scores is never a good thing.

8. **If at all possible, as far as it depends on you, live at peace with everyone. Do not take revenge, but leave room for God's wrath for it is written: "It is mine to repay", says the Lord.** Enough said!

My brothers can you answer this <u>Help Wanted Ad</u>? The Word says that the harvest is plentiful but the laborers are few. It is clear, given the time we are in, that there is a desperate need for emotionally and spiritually mature mentors. We need Christian employees resolved to help and not intentionally hurt fellow workers or in any way violate the charge they are called to carry out. God is calling for workers that will not moan and complain by the water cooler or take excessive breaks all the while scheming for extra fringe benefits but refusing to pay the cost of discipleship.

Don't think just because you are a hard worker on your earthly job that this will automatically qualify you to excel in your spiritual job. After all people do strange things in the secular work place and still manage to move up the ladder of success. This should not be so in the sacred world where workers are held to a higher standard. If a worker or department in the business world fails to live up to expectations, workers may be fired. If a worker in the Christian world fails to live up to expectations there may be a different firing in store if the behavior is not sincerely rectified.

One of the great fringe benefits working for the Lord, and unmatched by any job on Earth, is the impartation of The Holy Spirit. Every qualified worker can be covered. No one is left out of the plan. The Holy Spirit is not controlled by an earthly boss. The Holy Spirit has the power to renew your mind, heart and soul. It can make you a better person in the world and a more complete worker in the vineyard. The work of Kingdom building calls for Holy Ghost filled workers who will venture forth to transform pain into joy, hopelessness into faith and let the lost know they can be found. If you feel qualified, be of good cheer because God is calling. Help Wanted!

MENTOR'S MISSION FUEL
ARE YOU THE PROBLEM OR SOLUTION?

I attended Howard University in the turbulent 60's. I graduated on time much to the wonder of my peers. It was a fascinating era to be alive. Almost everywhere you turned, there was something meaningful (or with the potential to become meaningful) happening on big campus and around the country. There were student takeovers, boycotts; freedom rides; sit-ins, marches, along with some of the best speeches and concerts delivered by young movers and shakers (many whom are still moving and shaking).

The Howard faculty engrained in students the need to go back to the communities we hailed from and make it a better place. Now, I am not going to 'front' like every student was down with the cause because that would be far from the truth. Some of my brothers and sisters were down with other causes like: playing Bid, lyin' and lovin', drinkin' and druggin', failin' and wailin'. School and life is indeed about choices, and make no mistake, you will be held accountable for the choices you make and/or the choices you fail to make.

Speaking of choices, allow me to pose a 'back-in-the day' binary question that still has power today: "Are you part of the problem or part of the solution?" Unfortunately, there are many ways that people either knowingly, or unwittingly, becomes part of the problem. The 'playaz' who insist on hurting women become the problem when they leave a long string of broken-hearted sisters who vow never to trust another man. There can be no love without trust. The person who spends most of their waking hours in a self-induced haze caused by alcohol and drugs become the problem because they are stuntin' and bluntin' their potential and future. Many in my generation thought it possible to find a separate reality (ode to Carlos Castaneda) while high on mind-altering substances like marijuana, LSD, peyote or other hallucinogenic drugs. Whatever truths that were found during this period were often amusing, sometimes insightful but in the end, transitory and did not stand the test of time. The social, political, economic and moral problems that my generation faced are still causing problems today with one major difference. It is harder to find people who really care about the plight of others left behind.

We need more problem-solvers who are down with the community; who are strategic thinkers/doers, caring and strong. The decision to educate yourself also carries a responsibility to care about the welfare of the broader community, no matter your chosen major or eventual field of endeavor. I am not of the mindset that the only way to do 'good in the hood' is by staying and working in the 'hood'. Some of you will stay and some of you will not. But if you stay, leave, or come back to visit make a decision to do something that arrests the pain and suffering experienced by brothers and sisters caught in the vice-like grip of generational poverty, low ambition and depressing despair. Whatever you decide to do, please do not become separated from people in need by any capricious thoughts of privilege and status differences heaped upon you by institutions, businesses and individuals who are better served if you become blind to your true purpose and calling to be a liberator and elevator of poor and oppressed people.

Please don't join the ranks of other materialistic, superficial, bourgeois/'churcheoisie,' uncaring individuals who cannot see past their blessings, needs or problems in order to help others. Some of you grew up in families that had to struggle to send you to college, while others, well, 'ya got it like dat'. It does not matter if you are a have or were a have not, you must search deep inside yourself and decide how you are going to spend the rest of your life. I hope and pray you will make a conscious decision to use your time, talent and treasure to make a better world for yourself, family, friends and community. Brothers, you have a tremendous opportunity to do wonderful things; so as we use to say back in the day: Seize the time! Are you the problem or are you a problem solver? And as any good Bid Whist player knows: 'If you think long you think wrong!'

Questions to Ponder

1. Do you remember when you decided to become part of the solution rather than be the problem? What prompted your change?

2. Can you recall something that you did to help someone in need that can never be put on your resume?

3. What would you say to brothers with time, talent and treasure but are too busy with their grind to help others in need?

THE JOSHUA PARADOX: INTER-GENERATIONAL MENTORING AND LEADERSHIP DEVELOPMENT

By Jeremy Del Rio

Jeremy co-founded and directs 20/20 Vision for Schools, a movement to transform public education that launched in New York City in 2008; teaches as an adjunct faculty member at Alliance and Fuller seminaries; and connects, trains, and mentors youth workers through various youth development networks. He has consulted ministries and nonprofits since 2000, and directed Generation Xcel, a holistic youth center in Manhattan, from 1996-2006. Jeremy was the founding youth pastor at Abounding Grace Ministries (1994-2004), and also worked as a corporate attorney in New York. He has contributed to six books, including Deep Justice in a Broken World (Zondervan/YS 2008) and The Justice Project (Baker Books 2009), and his articles have appeared in Charisma, Willow, The Journal of Student Ministries, Relevant, and elsewhere. He and his wife Diana have two sons, Judah and Cyrus. Visit them online at www.JeremyDelRio.com.

A pastor from a major city serves faithfully for over forty years, plants a church that becomes a respected institution with several thousand members, raises up scores of leaders who would go on to shape ministry in the city for decades, and retires [from] the pastorate to serve as president of a Bible College. Most leaders would read this profile and aspire to something like it. It contains the elements of a great story: longevity, fruitfulness, influence, and legacy. The only thing missing is the details. Ah, the details. That's where the devil lurks, isn't it? Beneath the surface lies the murkiness that makes this story a bit more complicated. For all the leaders this pastor groomed, an all too common trait emerged. Rather than embrace his protégés and commission them, as Christ did, to do greater works than he, he seemed threatened by their rise and intimidated by their gifts.

Too often, this perceived threat grew into an unhealthy estrangement between teacher and student. When the pastor resigned, he left his church in chaos. No clear successor or team of successors created a leadership vacuum that sent the church into a tailspin. Nearly two decades later, the church survives, but only after years of unnecessary hardship and struggle. Called different things in different contexts - poor succession planning, power tripping, paranoia, bad discipleship, generation gap, ignorance - this scenario is not uncommon, nor is it reserved for the pastorate. It plays itself out all over the country in countless contexts. Yet a new generation of leaders needs mentors, role models, fathers, and spiritual disciple-makers - people who will invest in their lives, not because of what they can get, but for what they can give.

The Moses-Joshua relationship embodies this. Appointed by God to deliver His people from slavery, Moses understood early on that someone else would lead them into freedom. He recognized the need to "commission Joshua, and encourage and strengthen him, for [Joshua] will lead this people across and will cause them to inherit the land." (Deut. 3:27) As a result, Moses brought Joshua everywhere, exposed him to the deeper truths, introduced him to intimacy with God, empowered growth, and supported him through difficulty.

When Moses visited with God on Mount Sinai, the only other person permitted on the mountain was Joshua. (Ex. 24:13) At the Tent of Meeting, where Moses and God spoke "face to face," he brought Joshua. (Ex. 33:11) After deputizing Joshua to lead a militia against a band of dessert raiders, Moses provided spiritual cover from a nearby hilltop. As long as his hands remained upraised, Joshua prevailed. When he tired and dropped his arms, Joshua lost ground. (Ex. 17:9-14)

When it came time to preview the Promised Land, Moses sent Joshua and just eleven others. (Num. 13) When Joshua overstepped his bounds, Moses provided correction. (Num. 11:26-30) After investing in Joshua for forty years, Moses could confidently expect him to fulfill his destiny and lead the people out of the wilderness that Moses himself could not escape. Sadly, Joshua is a paradoxical figure. For as much benefit as he received from his mentor,

Joshua failed to reproduce the investment. He got along great with his peers. Men like Caleb and the other community elders served with Joshua as a great team, and even provided leadership for the people after his death. But Joshua's spiritual legacy did not survive a single generation. The book of Judges opens with one of the most distressing cautionary tales that too few contemporary leaders seem to understand. "After [Joshua's] generation had been gathered to their fathers, another generation grew up, who knew neither the Lord nor what he had done for Israel. Then the Israelites did evil ... [and] forsook the Lord." (Judges 2:10-12)

Today, as a new generation of young people is beginning to understand the plans and purposes God has for them, many of them are crying out for mentors. Will they find a Moses to embrace them, guide them, and encourage them to greatness? Or will they find a Joshua, someone too busy fulfilling his own destiny to invest in someone else's?

CHAPTER TWO

MENTOR'S INSIGHT IQ

"Why do you look at the speck of sawdust in your brother's eye and pay no attention to the plank that is in your own eye? You hypocrite, first take the plank out of your own eye, and then you will see clearly to remove the speck from your brother's eye." Matthew7: 3, 5

The beginning of my inner-liberation began when this word was seeded in me: "*Never allow your personal smallness to get in the way of your spiritual greatness.*" This Word is focused on the reality that spirit and flesh live side-by-side in all of us and exerts a daily ongoing tension that must be managed. But before this tension can be managed it must be recognized and understood. It is easy to chalk up bad habits, negative modes of behavior or excuse personal excess by saying, "This is just the way I am." This laissez-faire attitude toward personal smallness has crippled many men. The sad thing is that some brothers have grown accustom to limping.

When personal smallness becomes the only response to irritating situations, or people, it is difficult to escape from the penitentiary of self. Personal smallness can start off as a preference and grow into a lifestyle. It is the seemingly innocuous nature of this habit that makes it hard to see or eradicate. As personal smallness grows spiritual greatness is diminished.

The vision tool I would like to use to illustrate this point is a see-saw (or teeter-totter). When personal smallness is up spiritual greatness is down. Some children get excited when a perfect balance is struck on the see-saw and one can hang in mid-air indefinitely. The real excitement should be when Spiritual greatness stays up in the air. It is amazing that something as great and powerful as God's imparted Spirit can be diminished by personal smallness.

I soon discovered the second gift given to me was developing the courage to ask this penetrating question: "Lord is it really me?" This simple query allows one to take an unblinking look at self before pointing an accusing finger at others. The question is it really me, is the vehicle for personal reflection that if consistently and honestly practiced will lead to insight. Insight is the desire and ability to take a critical and honest look at self.

It is amazing how many people go through life seeing only the flaws, faux pas or foolishness of others. The plight of no insight is more than a catchy phrase. It is a malady that allows "excuse exits" to magically appear when personal responsibility is called for. The spiritually blind man will NEVER see himself as wrong but will be quick to cite wrong in others. This same person has a hard time confronting himself because he refuses to ask is it really me? Who would think that a simple four word question could open up an invisible door that leads inward?

Look at what the question can do for the man brave enough to ask, "is it really me pushing my pain on others because I am still in pain? Is it really me causing confusion because I am confused? Is it really me withholding praise and affection because I never received praise and affection? Is it really me causing the problems I am trying to fix? Is it really me who has a bad temper and not people who make me angry?" Without insight, these penetrating questions will never be truthfully answered.

Insight coupled with wisdom (mother wit/common sense) and tied to the Holy Spirit is a powerful transformative gift that orders a mentor's thoughts, aligns his steps and serves as an inner mirror for deep personal reflection. But going inside of oneself, while admirable, is not enough. The courage to deal with what is present is essential.

If a man looks at his inner brokenness and says, "Oh too bad I am broken" and willingly leaves the mess on the floor of his soul, what good was the inward journey? It must be said that men are not encouraged to be introspective. It is thought that women ask questions that shed light on their interior world while men stay focused on action that orders their exterior world. Society has helped men stay emotionally blind by sayings like: Big boys don't cry or never let them see you sweat. Even popular media capitalizes on men's emotional separation. The Terminator movies capture an interesting fusion between man and machine. The cyborg had no compassion and dispatched its prime directive with impunity. Men, we are not robots even though at times we respond robotically to issues calling for inner reflection.

Our adversary waits until the opportune time to bring up confusing/painful unresolved inner issues that one has either ignored or is convinced he can handle on his own. It is precisely at this time that all hell can break loose. The collateral damage injures the mentor who refuses to look inside for the source of trouble as well as hurt the trusting mentee. This is a high price to pay for the mentor, mentee and ministry. If you want to be a transformative mentor it is imperative that you take an inward journey and deal with guarded and potentially destructive issues before trying to address similar problematic issues in others.

Questions to Ponder

1. What thoughts were triggered for you after reading this Chapter? Based on these thoughts (or feelings) what are you willing to start doing and what are you willing to stop doing?

2. Think about a time someone gave you unsolicited feedback about yourself. What did they say and how did you receive it?

3. Can you give an example of how your personal smallness got in the way of your spiritual greatness?

MENTOR'S SPIRITUAL REFLECTION
STANDUP MAN FOR CHRIST
2Cor 6:1-10

In the movies about the mob, there is a term that is used to denote the type of person that will always do the right thing. This person puts loyalty first and will not turn on his benefactors. This man is called a standup guy. Now I want to take this reference away from mob association and drop it squarely into the text to investigate the making of a Standup Man for Christ. If there was ever a standup man for Christ it was The Apostle Paul.

Take a look at his resume. The first thing you may notice was that Paul was not always Paul. Just like most of us, Paul had a nefarious past covered under the name of Saul. Saul was a standup man for the Pharisees. He rose to the top of the pecking order through hard work and great intellect. He was the prized student of Gamaliel, an extremely gifted Chief Pharisee and teacher.

Saul was born a Roman citizen which afforded him rights that his Jewish colleagues did not have. After mastering the Law he saw as his life's purpose to zealously persecute members of the newfound movement called The Way (Christians). Saul was a standup guy motivated by what he thought was his mission and that was to be a living, breathing nightmare to those who dared to confess Jesus as their Savior. We read at the end of Acts 7 how Saul stood nearby and watched over the cloaks of elders as they stoned Stephen to death.

Saul had a lucrative profession as a tentmaker. He was able to take care of his needs and no doubt lived a comfortable lifestyle–say upper middleclass. He was multilingual and readily communicated with Greeks, Romans, Jews, philosophers, mystics and the common man. Saul was also a disciplined thinker and great writer (he wrote in flawless Greek). Saul with his natural standup gifts, talents, abilities and desire was standing for the wrong master. The transition from Saul to Paul may be to the ear the difference of one letter. His transformation was much deeper than that because the job he had to do was deeper than anything in his life up to this point. His name change from Saul the destroyer and persecutor to Paul the builder and preserver reflects the observable transformative process that anyone must make who is called to make a stand for Christ.

Saul had to suffer in order to become Paul. He was struck blind and could no longer function in the world he once knew. He had to suffer and be brought low in order to eventually stand tall. Let's look at what Paul had to endure as part of his transformation from a man standing up and immersed in the world into a man standing up and immersed in Jesus.

1. As mentioned Saul went through a conversion experience on The Damascus Road. He had to

become blind to the natural world so that he could see into the supernatural world. Talk about corrective vision!

2. As a Standup Man for Christ Paul had to develop a rich prayer life. He had to stay focused. He had to have a thick skin because he was challenged by the Roman government, by Pharisees, and ridiculed because of his diminutive stature. Paul had to learn valuable lessons from his 'thorn in the flesh' to accomplish what he was called to do.

3. Paul had to stand up in the midst of people in and out of the church. Some of the worst persecution (what goes around comes around) was from believers who remembered him well before his conversion. Paul suffered the scorn from the 'I remember you when' crowd.

Brothers, if you are going to be a Standup Man for Christ there are some things that you must do and some things you should expect. Here are some thoughts gleaned from the lesson:

1. A Standup man must never put stumbling blocks in the paths of others (vs. 3). He does not

delight in the downfall of brothers and sisters nor is he expected to knock people down.

2. A Standup man must expect to endure trials and tribulations: Let's hear from Paul in terms of what he went through to get through (2 Corinthians 11:23-29).

3. A Standup man must weather the storms of life and receives a different type of reward (vs. 6-7) namely: purity, patience, and understanding.

4. A Standup man must learn how to proactively and successfully deal with life's contradictions (vs. 8-10) and not be deterred or consumed by the same.

Make no mistake these are difficult lessons to comprehend let alone endure. It is easier to lie down in the gutter with the crowd than make a truthful and valiant stand, alone, for Christ. In these days, wrong has been twisted and made to appear right and right has been trampled and seems wrong. God has a track record for selecting standup men. Take a look through the Hall of Fame of Standup Men.

> • *He chose Moses who stammered but was able to stand up against mighty Pharaoh and manage to say:*

*"This is what the LORD, the God of Israel says:
'Let my people go.' "*
Exodus 5:1a

- He picked Joshua who stood up to the entire Israelite community and made this bold declaration:

"Now fear the Lord and serve him with all faithfulness... But if serving the Lord seems undesirable to you then chose for yourselves this day whom you will serve,... But as for me and my household we will serve the Lord."
Joshua 24: 14a, 15a

- He chose Shadrach, Meshach and Abednego and after being threatened by a fiery death by King Nebuchadnezzar, they refused to bow down and stood up saying:

"... If we are thrown into the blazing furnace, the God we serve is able to save us from your hand O King. But even if he does not, we want you to know, O King that we will not serve your gods or worship the image of gold you have set up."

* He chose David who throughout his checkered life made this memorable stand pleading:

"Create in me a clean heart O God, and renew a steadfast spirit in me. Do not cast me from your presence or take your Holy Spirit from me. Restore to me the joy of your salvation and grant me a willing spirit, to sustain me. Then I will teach transgressors your ways and sinners will turn back to you."
Psalm 51:10-13

The Lord has chosen stand up men to meet the challenges of the time. He can use men that others reject. He chose you and will give power from on high to help you stand with others who fell down and could not get back up. Are you a Standup Man for Christ?

MENTOR'S MISSION FUEL
IS THERE A HEALER IN THE HOUSE?

Excerpt from a Black History Month speech given to The National Association of Black Social Workers. I thank Carter G. Woodson for pressing his dream to celebrate the accomplishments of Black people.

I have been blessed to travel to just about every state in The Union. I have been way up high in the Rockies and way down low near the Mississippi Delta. I have been around the world giving a message of hope, perseverance and power. I have worked with young people on track and off track. I have heard the cries from economically well-off and from the hard-pressed poor. I have spoken to crowds in the thousands in convention centers and consoled a grandmother in a project basement lamenting the fact that no one showed up for a community meeting she called. I am not here to call out names etched on the Black History Hall of Fame. As a Civil War and Reconstruction major at Howard University, I can do that. But I am led in a different direction and that is to talk to people who have the power to shape history by ensuring that people are not done in by history.

There is an enemy that has been stalking communities and families for generations. It is not The KKK or The White Citizens Council. Don't get me wrong, I know racism is unfortunately alive and well. What I am talking about are the relentless and remorseless attacks to mind, body and spirit of our people of all ages and socio-economic backgrounds. That is why I am here beloved on one of my more important assignments given to me. I want to offer it to you as we draw near to the close of Black History month to ask this question: Is There A Healer In The House? I want to borrow a page from Dr. Joy DeGruy

Leary's thesis in her landmark book titled *Post-traumatic Slave Syndrome.* It is clear that many families today have not recovered from the generational attacks that have kept some in poverty and in families riddled with physical, emotional and sexual trauma. That is why the call must go out to Healers.

Generational poverty has been exacerbated by individual, family and community destruction caused by Crack. This drug, a derivative of Cocaine, was diabolically aimed at women and children. Slavery, with all of its viciousness, could not break the mother/child bond but Crack, in a matter of weeks did that and much more! Beloved, my message is clear, direct and I pray challenging. Is There A Healer In The House? Self-hatred and low self-esteem have colluded to stifle the creativity and abort the destiny of young and not-so young. Generational poverty has mired some of our brothers and sisters in what seems like an unbreakable caste system. As the rich get richer the poor are getting poorer. Their sad legacy is to forever live in cold and impoverished shadows in a land rich with light.

Is There A Healer In The House?

The absence of fathers in the home has geometrically increased the pressure on single female-headed households. Boys are growing up without fathers and are birthing children that in many instances will not know their fathers. Boys without fathers grow up to be men without fathers. This cycle must be broken.

Is There A Healer In The House?

Returning citizens (I dropped saying ex-offenders) leaving the prison system need help reintegrating with themselves, family and society. The number of people of all ages and gender doing time is increasing exponentially in what has been called modern day slavery (Read *The New Jim Crow* by Michelle Alexander).

Is There A Healer In The House?

We need healers that will share their knowledge and will strengthen formal and informal programs to help those in need.

1. We need healers to lead efforts in houses of worship ministering to the needs of young people and their families who are victims of miseducation, drugs and senseless violence. The faith community is blessed with professionals that have a commitment, mandate and Spirit to serve that is best captured in the scripture: 'What you do for the least of these you do also unto me...'

2. We need healers who can strengthen efforts and interventions that protect a child from living marginal lives, or sadly, committing suicide. That same child living in poverty or contemplating

ending his or her life could very well grow up and become a healer destined to set captives free.

3. We need healers who help families so children do not have to enter the foster care system. Healers who will help kinship foster care providers with a special assist to grandparents raising grandchildren. While kinship foster care is an extension of the extended family model honored in our history and culture this reconstituted family concept could benefit from targeted assistance and policy change.

4. We need healers to respectfully help elders adjust to aging and thereby truly honor the history our ancestors were able to make. This present era is ruled by marketers, businesspersons and entrepreneurs driven to push youth as the only stage of life that counts. Meanwhile our elders who built strong families, communities, churches, and spoke truth to power, are largely ignored and deemed irrelevant.

History moves on a pendulum. We have had some prosperous years and now we are moving deep into the lean years. These lean years will exact a toll on families already reeling from real or benign neglect. There is more pressure on inadequately funded schools in poor neighborhoods that continue to be the conveyor belt from the community straight to prison. The downward economy has disproportionately impacted poor people and has been unkind to teens and men of color evidenced by a near 50% unemployment rate. So healers make sure you take care of yourself. As you know this work can burn you up and take you out. Make sure you do what refreshes your mind, body and spirit. Don't be a 24/7 social worker. If you have a hobby or a talent, don't neglect it. I thank God for your families. They most probably never went to social work school, but have heard enough cases from you to qualify for a degree. I know they have been the wind beneath your wings but you must not burn them out.

It is gratifying to have this opportunity to talk to trained healers. It is imperative that your collective counseling skills break out of the silo of specialization and find people on the battlefield struggling to address issues that out distance their ability to properly respond. You can teach 'survival' social work skills to untrained brothers and sisters toiling on the frontlines with youth and families. You can assist sisters and brothers helping to bring order to families riven by domestic violence. You can help the child suffering from low-self-esteem or diagnosed with ADHD. You can be answered prayers to the plea: *Is There A Healer In The House?*

MENTOR'S TESTIMONY
TRANSFORMING TONY THE TIGER
By Derek H. Suite, M.D. M.S.

Dr. Derek Suite is a board certified psychiatrist. He is co-founder, president and medical director of an award winning multidisciplinary, community mental health practice called Full Circle Health PLLC. His practice incorporates psycho-spiritual counseling techniques (medication when necessary) as a foundational method of intervention. Dr. Suite is the Northeast and Mid-Atlantic representative for the Black Psychiatrist of America (BPA). He and his wife co-authored a marriage/couple enrichment book titled Fruit of the Spirit, Thorns In The Flesh. Dr. Suite is an elder on the ministerial staff of Circle of Christ Church.

Mentoring Tony was not easy. He hated taking instructions and did not like being corrected on anything. At the same time, he wanted my advice, approval, and blessing on almost every mad-capped idea or quirky project he got into. Seeing that he was trouble, I initially told him to find another person to mentor him. After all, I was busy and had little time to argue with some pushy kid over the implausibility of his dreams and schemes. Obviously resourceful and resistant, Tony, upon seeing that I wanted nothing to do with him, befriended my wife and worked with her just so that he could remain in the orbit. This strategy worked. She would repeatedly ask me to help him commenting, *"he is such a nice boy."* I was now in a no win situation against formidable wife pressure. Reluctantly, I took him on and allowed him to work alongside me.

An immediate practice I instituted was meeting with Tony to give critical feedback each time we worked on a project together. This "feedback session" was not a fun experience to say the least. He struggled with my brutal honesty around his personal and professional conduct. I could see him boiling when I told him I did not like what he was wearing, or how he spoke, or that his work performance was subpar. Tony complained bitterly to others that I simply could not be pleased. Feedback meetings between us would be tense with him giving very little eye contact or at times glaring. When I was done with my laundry list of problems, I would often invite him to speak. His having no comment only magnified our already antagonistic relationship.

When he could no longer take it, Tony would flare up and dare to confront: *"You just don't see what I do as good,"* he would gush. *"I don't have to take this. My people tell me that I am being treated like a slave. You call me at any hour of the night and expect me to respond. You ask me to do a million things, and if I get one thing wrong, you are on my case. This is driving me crazy. I can't do this anymore."* Silently, I would listen as Tony manned up. I tried very hard to conceal my unspeakable joy. "Could this be it," my inner voice would whisper, "Yes! He is finally outta here." But to my shock and chagrin, Tony, would, without fail, make a full about face seconds after he spewed: *"Hey doc, I'm sorry man. I don't know what just got into me just now. I was just thinking about so many things. I know this is right for me. I don't want to leave. I know I said some things but please don't get rid of me. Just give me a chance. I want this process."*

What was I supposed to do with this, I often thought? What could I do but say, "Okay Tony, no problem but don't put yourself through this. We can still be cool with each other even if we don't work together." He would never fall for my not so subtle attempt to show him the door even after he straightened up. *"No, that's okay,"* he would say reaching out to shake my pocketed hand. *"You will see I will get this thing right. I will make you proud."* This scene would replay itself at least once a month over a two year span. I guess doing it so often finally taught me that what Tony, who had lost his father to a fatal car accident, was looking for was connection to a father figure at all costs. Once I became attuned to this, I was less inclined to get him out of my life — not that he would permit it anyway. By the third year of mentorship, I would start feedback exchanges by reassuring him saying, "This is not about getting rid of you. I see your potential and your promise but I have to tell you that..." I could see him sitting and absorbing what I was saying. It wasn't that he agreed with everything but he learned how to take the coaching. I secretly admired his ability to do that.

By year four, the trust between us grew. I would call on him to handle sensitive projects for me and he would generally perform with excellence. Tony showed an uncanny ability to anticipate what I needed. If I didn't know better I would think he studied me and my habits in detail. After his demonstrated excellence in so many areas, I lightened up and stopped giving feedback sessions. Interestingly, Tony would hunt me down for critical feedback. When I told him I had nothing to say he would bring up times he 'messed' up in the past and want to go over what I said back then, often adding that he did not appreciate what I was communicating until now.

One day it finally hit me that I was in the middle of this young man's transformation process. I witnessed Tony transform himself from a wayward, resistant, child into a mature young man who wants to learn from doing, having contact with elders, and hearing about his mistakes. I knew that this transformation was in full swing when my wife overheard Tony, now 22, holding a feedback meeting with some of his friends after a party that they recently had. She said he was being really tough with them. When I asked her what she meant she said he told the group they are free to leave if they don't want his feedback. I laughed hard upon hearing this but also came to understand how special Tony was to have withstood my pressure and take the best parts of what I had offered him and actively incorporate it into his life.

Questions to Ponder

1. Did you ever mentor a "difficult" mentee; what was the experience like for you and for the mentee?

2. What part of Tony did you see in yourself?

3. Would you have taken on this difficult challenge or would you have looked for an easier mentee to lead and guide?

CHAPTER THREE

MENTOR'S HURT LOST BOY

*Why are you so downcast, O my soul? Why so
disturbed within me?
Psalm 42:5a*

Prayerfully after gaining insight and working on character issues, there will come a time when a man called to mentor will have a compelling desire to find his inner hurt lost boy that was left behind as the man grew up. If the truth be told, that boy, though often neglected, has played a major role in shaping the man. How can this be? My brother if you want to know the man you have become you must be willing to take an unblinking look at the hurt lost boy inside of you. Your hurt lost boy learned very early in life how to deal with rejection and disappointments. The easiest way for him to cope with life disappointments was to learn how to cry inside. The process for a man emotionally shutting down does not happen when he starts dating or after getting married. The hurt lost boy knows, sometimes better than the man, why and when emotional avoidance and manhood merged.

So one learns at an early age how to excuse, overlook or avoid painful emotions. Some say it is nurture others say it is nature; both can lead to a low emotional I.Q. supported by societal norms. The expectation that most men (hear "real" men) are alienated from their feelings is accepted in many quarters as fact. The hurt lost boy in you has retreated into your inner-self protected by the pit bulls of denial and fear. The grown man has become adept at keeping even well-intentioned people away from the boy so he cannot reveal damaging secrets. Direct questions that can unmask his whereabouts are skillfully evaded, met with stony silence, or rebuffed by an angry self-protecting (boy protecting) tirade.

Over time the man learns how to make man-size excuses for the little boy's pain. He says things like: It didn't really hurt when his father said he would come by and never showed up or called. It didn't really hurt when your high school girlfriend (first love) called it quits. It really did not hurt as you watched your parent's addiction kill the joy that used to be in the house. It did not really hurt to see how death slowly and painfully took a loved one away. It did not really hurt when you were molested. It did not really hurt when you saw the latest man in your house beat on your mother. It didn't really hurt and guess what - the pain never really went away. The hurt lost boy knows all, sees all and tells nothing. All of this emotion packed deep inside of a man impacts what is said, heard and felt in interactions that have nothing to do with past pain. This emotional bundle takes a great deal of energy to keep under wraps. This is probably one of several reasons women live longer than men. Unfortunately this energy sometimes explodes-usually at the worst time.

It is time to go find your hurt lost boy. The same steps you would take to mentor a boy assigned to you are similar steps you can follow when dealing with your inner boy. You have to want to help him. There must be trust and respect. Don't be angry with him when you find him. This will make him retreat to a deeper, darker place within you. Don't accuse him. Don't make him feel guilty. Don't deny his pain. Don't dismiss him. Don't laugh at him. Don't act like he is not you. You have to know that the act of talking to the boy does not diminish your manhood. You have to want to meet that boy more than half way. In fact you have to diligently seek him. The hurt lost boy can tell you things about you that you may not want to hear or accept. He knows why you act or react the way that you do especially in tense and or emotional situations. The hurt lost boy was present before the man appeared. The boy can be your best friend or worse enemy. The choice is yours. If you want to man up, get up and go look for the hurt lost boy. And when you find him, love him.

Questions to Ponder

1. If you could talk to the hurt lost boy inside of you how would you start the conversation?

2. What would be the hardest thing for you to hear or say?

3. What price have you paid by not dealing with your hurt lost boy?

You may find that this search has stirred up issues that may be too difficult to handle on your own. If that is the case, I strongly recommend that you talk to your Pastor or to a skilled therapist equipped to help you navigate your inward journey. Healing is both a rewarding and difficult process; and please remember, there is nothing unmanly about asking for help if you need it.

MENTOR'S SPIRITUAL REFLECTION
LIVING WITH A HURT THAT WON'T HEAL
John 5:1-9

John is the fourth book of The Gospels. It is not part of the Synoptic Gospels because of its unique literary form, structure and purpose. John is thought to be written by the "disciple that Jesus loved." It is an undisputed theological treatise with this unique opening:

> **In the beginning was the Word and Word was with God and the Word was God. John 1:1**

John goes on to say:

> **...these are written that you believe that Jesus is the Christ, the Son of God, and that believing you may have life in His name. John 20: 31**

John also contains one of the most quoted scriptures. It is so well known that one can just say John 3:16 and *most* church folk know:

For God so loved the world that He gave his only son that whosoever believe in Him shall not die but have eternal life.

Other distinguishing characteristics of John from the Synoptic Gospels are different miracle accounts. John is built around eight miracles. The first was when Jesus turned water into wine at the wedding at Cana. John is the only reporter of Jesus' encounter with the Samaritan woman he met at the well. But it is the miracle found in John 5 that fascinates me and will serve as our scripture focus. The text gives an account of a man that had a hurt that for the previous 38 years would not heal. The text states that he was an invalid, a cripple if you will. He could not do what most people could do for themselves. His physical hurt was visible for all to see. Men, this pericope inspires talking about a different type of hurt that is not physical. I am talking about an invisible emotional hurt that causes visible behavioral problems.

This hurt influences a sufferer's personality, attitude and impacts other key dimensions of life. Before we go deeper it is important that all are on the same page by admitting we have either been hurt or we have hurt other people. Some men carry invisible wounds throughout their life. The pain can manifest in the home, on the job, with family members and YES even in the church. This emotional hurt could have been intentionally inflicted or could have been unintentional. The resulting hurt could be carried for decades or the pain is fresh as yesterday's stinging words. It does not matter to the sufferer and the severity of damage may not be known to the person that inflicted the pain.

Now that we are all here let us go back to the text and see what we can learn from our central actor. We are not told much about the paralyzed man at the side of the pool except that he has been in this condition for 38 years. We don't know his name. We don't know his parent's name. We don't know where he lived. We don't know how old he was or when or how for that matter he became a paralytic. Was he born that way? Did he fall off of a camel and become paralyzed? What we can surmise is that his physical injury no doubt caused him emotional pain.

He probably wondered why me? When is this pain going to be over? Why won't God heal me? Who is going to bring me out here tomorrow? I am tired of being a burden. I am tired of begging. I am sick and tired of being sick and tired. Sounds familiar? There are brothers who have carried their emotional pain as long if not longer than 38 years. The hurt could have been inflicted during childhood by a family member. The pain could have been caused by a relationship that soured or from unrequited love. The hurt could stem from rejection, alienation, mental, physical or sexual abuse. The emotional pain could be the result of incessant teasing from childhood about a physical characteristic that has left an emotional scar.

Sometimes a man can overcompensate for his pain and resort to inflicting damage on others before damage can be inflicted on him. This is the premise of the bestselling book *Hurt People Hurt People.* Hurt people can hurt people even when they are trying to help people. It must be said that some people who inflict hurt are not aware of their hurting ways so the hurt just keeps on hurting. The reason this happens is that it is impossible to see yourself the way others see and experience you (review Mentor's Insight I.Q. if this sounds new).

God has an amazing system that helps physical hurts heal. When we are cut, the wound heals under a scab. Over time the scab falls off and the injury is healed. But if the scab is picked off or comes off before time, the hurt can be re-infected and the healing process must start all over. Just when we think we've got it together something is said, a song played, perfume smelled and we are back in that dark, painful and lonely place. We ask ourselves how long must we hurt? Some people try to take matters in their own hands and try to heal themselves through: drinking, drugging, binge eating, mindless shopping, a string of meaningless sexual encounters or becoming isolated and depressed.

The fortune of the man at the pool was about to change. He was about to have an encounter not with a tormentor, not with someone who would put a coin in his cup but with a healer like no other. When Jesus went over to the man he did not ask him embarrassing questions linked to his sad state. Jesus asked him one of the more profound questions given the reality of the man. He asked, "Do you want to be made well?" At first glance one could think what kind of question is that to ask a helpless man? Stepping back, the question makes all the sense in the world. Jesus and good counselors know that it is quite possible for a person in need of help to become comfortable in an uncomfortable situation. This is a good definition of a person content to be stuck in a rut. This unfortunate rut dweller finds creative ways to make excuses for being stuck and carrying on with his hurt. His pain moves from being a burden and over time morphs into becoming a responsibility.

So here is good news for anyone who wants to be made well. I am not talking about a temporary fix. I am not referring to a series of brief exits from the side of the pool only to return. I am not alluding to something you have to buy or stand in $1000 offering line in order to receive. I am talking about the same deal that was offered to the man by the pool. Jesus asked the man do you want to be made well? Before the man could answer Jesus gave this explicit direction.

1. **Get Up**. There is a personal responsibility to healing that cannot be ignored. This is not

magic. The Bible states IF you go, I will go with you. The two-letter word **IF** has stopped so many people. You have to get up and get past your IF.

2. **Pick Up** Pick up the divan of depression. Pick up your pity pillow you have wallowed on for years. Pick up that throw pillow of anger. Pick up the futon of foolishness. Pick up the sofa of self-satisfaction. Pick up the Lazy Boy you lazy boy.

3. **Walk Up.** Move away from the place of pain and brokenness because you won't be coming back. Not to visit. Not to reminisce. Not to claim. You are on your way to your destiny but you have to walk on your own to get there.

The place where the man laid for 38 years was called Bethesda. The Greek translation of Bethesda means House of Mercy. Today there is no pool where the waters are troubled but there is power being released right now. The church should be Bethesda for all who are physically hurting, or have become psychologically incapacitated by past slights, words or deeds. In order to be made well you may have to forgive the person who caused you pain. The more hurt you can jettison inside you on the way to being made well the more help and hope you can receive. Please don't make a little bit of room mind you, but as much as you can muster. Present your emptied space to the Lord. Do you want to be made well? Do you no longer want to live with a hurt that won't heal? It is time my brother to Get Up, Pick Up and Walk Up.

Questions to Ponder

1. At what point in time in your life could you best relate to the man by the side of the pool?

2. Looking back over your life how did you move from a situation that caused you pain to power?

3. What lessons can you take from this reflection that can help you and your mentee?

MENTOR'S MISSION FUEL
PERSONAL PUBLIC RELATIONS REVIEW

Each day our personal public relations department communicates ideas, emotion, intent, energy and spirit to the world-at-large. Intrapersonal bits and pieces of our inner/private core such as our: insecurity, fears, wants, doubts, angst, hopes, dreams, bad and/or good thoughts are continuously processed, packaged and communicated through direct and indirect "broadcast lines". Through these various modes of "transmissions", one communicates the inner essence of the real person.

It is a wonderful experience when your p.r. firm is performing at peak efficiency on your behalf. This means that messages from the inside of you are being clearly and consistently transmitted to the outside public. This consistency of thought, word and deed is recognized as your personality. There are words that can be easily found to describe you such as: steady, friendly, dependable, honest. You worked hard on yourself to become the person you always hoped to be and that is a noteworthy achievement.

It is quite the opposite experience when your inner p.r. company starts to freelance and sends out half-processed, hastily constructed, outdated or pulled from the inner back shelf messages that you do not wish to be made public or worse, you were not aware of a transmission occurring. Some people never review their personal public relations firm's performance. They are frequently misunderstood, constantly re-explaining themselves, or simply confused by why they cannot get what they think is their real persona across to others. The gap between what the message should be and what the message is creates a distorted picture that needs more halfhearted words to explain.

For example you say you are trustworthy but your eyes are still shifty, harkening back to your dicey days. The more you say you can be trusted, the more unbelievable you come across. The reality is that it is difficult to experience self in the same manner that others experience you. Thus compounding the difficulty when it is not clear which you is being projected-the old you or the new you? Another example of a personal p.r. gaffe happens when a man is delivered from let's say using drugs. In his mind he is clean and sober. What he cannot see is that he may still have negative residual ways learned on the street. This is evidenced by how he perceives the motives of others. His paranoid nature developed for years ago gets in the way of his ability to develop intimacy and trust. Even if you never used drugs there may be vestiges of your old character that seeps into your present interactions with others. This is true for former alcoholics, womanizers, the formally incarcerated or men who have been hurt in relationships.

It is possible to carry old hurts and pains into new situations and NOT BE AWARE that unresolved past issues can communicate messages through body language, or to the other extreme destructive self-sabotage. Now it is possible for you to be misread and it is not the fault of your p.r. firm but the inability of a person not understanding who you are or have other intentions or needs that are not known to you. This is what makes being real and being understood so difficult. I remember when a person I mentored got me wrong and communicated her thoughts that I got wind of. I confronted the person by saying, "If you believe I am the person that you described to your friend is really me I feel sorry for you because you have been around me all this time and you don't have a clue as to who I am."

Are you satisfied with your personal p.r. firm's performance on your behalf? Can you say with confidence the internal and external you are aligned and being consistently and truthfully communicated? This is an important consideration because it is impossible to change behavior one is not aware he is exhibiting. This is problematic for men who are not accustomed to hearing unsolicited feedback about themselves. If a critique is heard as an attack instead of constructive criticism, the hurt man's p.r. firm sinks into attack mode and cranks out negative energy couched in barbed words that cast deeper dispersion on the other person's character. It is important to be aware of what is being broadcast to others because what goes around comes around and unfortunately, can come back around again and again.

Questions to Ponder

1. Think of times/situations when your p.r. firm works well on your behalf. Recall a time when your firm miscommunicated the real you to others.

2. What is the easiest part of you to communicate (favorite attribute). What is the most difficult part of you to communicate (the hidden you).

3. Based on what you read and now understand what are you willing to start doing to represent yourself; and conversely, what are you willing to stop doing?

MENTOR'S MISSION FUEL
ADVICE TO A SINGLE MOM
By Rev. Din Tolbert M.Div.

Rev. Din Tolbert was on the ministerial staff of The Greater Allen A.M.E. Cathedral of New York where he served as Pastor of Shekinah Youth Chapel. He grew up in Allen participating in many of the programs he once managed. Rev. Tolbert graduated from Cornell University and received his M.Div. from Union Theological Seminary in 2010.

As a matter of context, it is important to state that Rev. Din Tolbert's contribution is in response to an email sent by a single mom asking for "manly/fatherly" advice for her son. While the request was forwarded to prominent brothers in the fatherhood and mentoring movement, it was telling that the youngest man, who was not a father, was the only responder.

Here is the mother's email (she gave permission to reproduce it) that spurred Rev. Din Tolbert's thoughtful and heartfelt response.

I need a helpful word from friends. Here is my story. This last weekend Asa and I were out and about. I thought we had a good time. At least I did! I am abiding by most of the 8- year-old masculine rules that Asa has set in place for me. Which includes not be able to kiss him within a two block radius of his school, not walking him into the school but stopping at the corner and as he walks up to the school pretending as if I am not watching him get safely inside and chilling about the amount of food he eats (more like nibbles). I am flexible because he is a good person. He is obedient, kind and hardworking when he puts his mind to it. So we get home and he says to me, "Mom it is hard for me to see other kids with their dads. You know a boy is not a boy without a dad." Those were his exact words. I was so shocked at how clearly he spoke to me that I fumbled my answer. It was something to the effect that he still had a dad, just that his dad was sick with diabetes and did not live with us… And also he had a heavenly Father. Asa gave me a sad sort of sigh and a dutiful, "yes mom."

Four days later I am still pained by his words. I remember being the age he is. It is when you discover your parents are fallible. I'm growing more aware that I see, hear and act on things from a female perspective. This perspective I know is limited so I would love to hear from people who were actually boys at one time or have sons. In desperation I am even checking out if there are any Father Knows Best reruns on YouTube. I know I need to come bigger on this one or my kid cred is about gone! Any suggestions and wisdom are welcome. Thank you!

Rev. Din's response:

I think that, if the masculine rules that you take notice of, are the result of a conversation between you and Asa, you've got a miracle of a young man on your hands who can articulate feelings and needs respectfully enough for them to be taken seriously and implemented into a parenting strategy. To have a child that intelligent [with a] desire to take the time to be vocal with you says to me that he has a vested interest in you parenting him well, and he'll work with you and trust your resources, whether they come out of your abundance or an honest grappling with your lack.

That being said, your "kid cred" is high enough that I think Asa would value honest conversation about what particular limitations you face as a single mother. If you have identified men in your life that you can vouch for character-wise, commitment-wise and capacity-wise (I suggest more than one man, of varying ages), I think Asa would be open to conversation about bringing trusted male figures into his life. They can be assigned different responsibilities - maybe one can be the guy who takes him to cultural events, another can be sporting events, etc.

Be very clear that these men are not trying to replace his father, but are helping you step in and provide male guidance for him because it is so important during these formative years of his life. I also think that his birth father should, if possible, play a part in Asa's life (please forgive me for assuming that he doesn't already).

I remember the age when I found out my parents (my father in particular) were not superheroes - a painful separation, moving with my mom from one NYC borough to another, my father dying from complications of AIDS, and one of the biggest, most humbling, and character defining experiences of that time was to see my hero father flawed. It gave me a real sense of my humanity and compassion for the humanity of others. He also imparted some of his sagest advice to me during that time, not that he was ever a proud secretive man, but there was a sense that the veil was torn, all bets were off and knowing that he would not be around for high school prom, graduation, college, my wedding prompted him to fast track some of his fatherly wisdom. I'm still eating at the table of what my father shared with me while dying an imperfect man's death.

At the end of the day, I believe Asa has articulated a need...and we see from society today that it is not a need that will go away as he gets older. He will seek out male influence to shape his understanding of himself in the world. I think that's a crucial shaping process and it behooves you to have your hands all up and in that! Lol.

Men of character, who will be committed and who represent the kind of attributes/world views/access that complement the wonderful work you already seem to be doing are key. They exist in enough obscurity that you may have to look for them, but in enough abundance that they will be found if you commit to the search. God bless you and I'm not at all opposed to being kept abreast of Asa's development as a young man of promise.

Question to Ponder

1. If you received this email what advice would you give to the mother of young Asa?

2. What thoughts do you have why men known for addressing the issues in the mother's email failed to respond?

3. What part of Rev. Din's response struck a nerve with you or made you say hmmmm?

MENTOR'S TESTIMONY
IS THIS THE KIND OF MAN I AM DESTINED TO BECOME?

By Brad Zervas

Brad Zervas is an award-winning leader, educator, activist and youth advocate. As a teacher, and more recently as an executive in the nonprofit sector, he has galvanized generations of young people through programs of his own design whose results have earned regional and national recognition. Brad began his career as a teacher, first at the Eaglebrook School and then at Northfield Mt. Hermon School in Massachusetts, two of the nation's most prestigious independent boarding schools. At the same time, he developed and ran a literacy program at a maximum security facility for men in Somers, Connecticut. The contrast between prison yard (razor-wire, lock-downs and concrete) and school yard (gardens, golden retrievers, blue blazers and summers in Maine) was acute-and indelible. But there were similarities between the groups—two isolated worlds marked by brutality, despair and denial. Troubled boys grow up to be troubled men, no matter what their economic backgrounds or family history, Brad quickly realized. In the next few years, as his understanding of childhood development deepened, so did his resolve to learn how to make a difference in the lives of boys and young men at risk. He joined The Boys' Club of New York, the nation's oldest and largest organization of its kind, in 1992, as the organization's Education Director. In 2000, he was appointed its Executive Director, only the sixth such appointment in the Club's 130-year history. His achievements at BCNY-and there are many-have brought Brad international recognition for his thought leadership, program development skills and writing talent. Brad launched The Ascension Project in 2009 to create a platform of advocacy for boys, and to provide a central source of information and ideas for a new generation of educators, social workers, advocates, and legislators, along with boys and their families, teachers and mentors. Brad was recently named Executive Director of Boys Hope Girls Hope of New York where he will over-see the organization's two urban boarding school programs in Brooklyn.

I remember when we first gathered the twenty-five thirteen and fourteen-year old boys who had been chosen to participate in a two-week leadership retreat in a remote area of the Bahamas. Their spirits were high and their own images of palm trees, resorts and beautiful beaches were enough to convince them that they were about to embark on a vacation generally afforded to the rich and famous. Their parents, who were also at this meeting, were clearly very proud and excited and while we did try and temper some of this, expectations can often distort the truth. Our goals were really quite simple. We wanted to challenge these boys and encourage them to consider what qualities were truly needed in order to become a good man.

While the boys certainly had their expectations, these were quickly replaced by a reality that they could not have possibly anticipated. The half hour ride from the airport to the school where they would be staying and studying revealed a countryside that was punctuated by large numbers of men idly standing and sitting by the roadside, houses in disrepair, barefoot women carrying buckets of water and other supplies, broken down cars and trucks and very little in the way of infrastructure. This was not the Bahamas they had imagined, but rather, an island with nearly 80 percent unemployment, little industry and a scarcity of fresh water. Once at school, they settled into their quarters and quickly learned that the heat would be oppressive and the bugs atrocious.

The volume that they were accustomed to have had been turned way down and what we all began to hear were the inner voices that we rarely shared with others. By the second week, we were experiencing emotional outbursts and patterns of behavior we had never witnessed before. While the group struggled to find its identity and achieve the sense of unity it so desperately needed, we were engaged in activities that required risk, cooperation, sharing and trust. The boys were not readily pre-disposed to such expressions and as their own masks began to peel away, we began to make progress.

Just three days before and during one of our leadership training sessions, we heard boys talk of fathers who were in prison, of some who had died and of others never known. When pressed to describe what they felt they would need to achieve to become men of honor and grace, many of the boys responded with observations that revealed both longing and understanding. They spoke about fatherhood and the need to care for family and community in ways that very few of them had witnessed first-hand yet they knew instinctively that there were lessons to be learned and a shortage of men to teach them these lessons.

Later that evening, one boy pulled me aside along with one of the counselors who had been traveling with us to tell us something he said he had never told anyone else. He told us about the day his father beat him and his mother senseless and then left only to return four years later to steal from them. In between, a succession of other men followed accompanied by more broken promises and unexpected departures. "Was this the kind of man I am destined to become?" he asked. "How can I trust you?" "Are you going to leave me when I need you most?" No boy should ever have to ask these kinds of questions and for those that need answers, we must continue to find ways to address their fears, provide meaning to their lives and convince them that by becoming good men, noble and strong, capable of tears and moments of weakness, of days of glory, service and need; we can find the new leadership we are currently lacking and strengthen our families, our communities and our nation.

CHAPTER FOUR

MENTOR'S 40 DEVELOPMENTAL ASSETS

But we have this treasure in earthen vessels...
2 Corinthians 4:7a (NKJV)

I was blessed to meet the late Dr. Peter L. Benson when he was President of The Search Institute in the early 1990's. The Search Institute is a youth development think tank with a national training arm. The heart of this organization's mission is met through research done to identify 40 Developmental Assets that all young people need in order to grow and thrive. The Search Institute's contention is the more assets a young person has the better outcomes one can expect in life.

The 40 Developmental Assets have been taught to youth workers, community, religious and civic leaders around the country, hailing from big states, little states, big cities, small cities and rural areas. The work of The Search Institute is not limited to this country. The developmental assets have traveled around the world. For more information about The Search Institute go online and check out www.searchinstitute.org.

Here is a list of the assets broken down in External and Internal domains. Successful mentors are able to help foster and/or integrate assets through building a solid relationship with their mentee. Other assets come from the family, community and institutions (i.e. schools, youth programs and houses of worship). It should be noted that most youth will not have all 40 assets listed. Research tells us that boys traditionally have fewer assets than girls. What we must do is see to it that young people get as many assets possible. It is important to say that mentors should ensure that their own children are asset rich before trying to improve assets in other people's children. You never want this saying to apply to you: The shoemaker's children have the worse shoes in town. How sad.

One of the weaknesses of many youth programs in the church is an absence of evaluation tools. The 40 Developmental Assets can offer a mentoring inventory checklist as well as a mentor diagnostic assessment tool. Proper interpretation of the assets can help tailor mentoring activities and behavioral recommendations according to the individual need of a young person. This action can also help a program not create a cookie cutter one size fits all strategy.

EXTERNAL ASSETS

Support

1. Family support—Family life provides high levels of love and support.

2. Positive family communications—Young person and his or her parent(s) communicate positively, and young person is willing to seek advice and counsel from parent(s).

3. Other adult relationships— Young person receives support from three or more nonparent adults.

4. Caring neighborhood—Young person experiences caring neighbors.

5. Caring school climate—School provides a caring, encouraging environment.

6. Parent involvement in schooling—Parent(s) are actively involved in helping young person succeed in school.

Empowerment

7. Community values youth—Young person perceives that adults in the community value youth.

8. Youth as resources—Young people are given useful roles in the community.

9. Services to others—Young person serves in the community one hour or more per week.

10. Safety—Young person feels safe at home, at school and in the neighborhood.

Boundaries and expectations

11. Family boundaries—Family has clear rules and consequences, and monitors the young person's whereabouts.

12. School boundaries—School provides clear rules and consequences.

13. Neighborhood boundaries—Neighbors take responsibility for monitoring young person's behavior.

14. Adult role models—Parent(s) and other adults model positive, responsible behavior.

15. Positive peer influence—Young person's best friends model responsible behavior.

16. High expectations—Parent(s) and teachers encourage the young person to do well.

Constructive use of time

17. Creative activities—Young person spends three or more hours per week in lessons or practice in music, theater, or the arts.

18. Youth programs—Young person spends three or more hours per week in sports, clubs and/or organizations at school or in the community.

19. Religious community—Young person spends one or more hours per week in activities in a religious institution.

20. Time at home—Young person is out with friends "with nothing special to do" two or fewer nights per week.

INTERNAL ASSETS

Commitment to learning

21. Achievement motivation—Young person is motivated to do well in school.

22. School engagement—Young person is actively engaged in learning.

23. Homework—Young person reports doing at least one hour of homework every school day.

24. Bonding to school—Young person cares about her or his school.

25. Reading for pleasure—Young person reads for pleasure three or more hours per week.

Positive values

26. Caring—Young person places high value on helping other people.

27. Equality and social justice—Young person places high value on promoting equality and reducing hunger and poverty.

28. Integrity—Young person acts on convictions and stands up for her or his beliefs.

29. Honesty—Young person "tells the truth even when it is not easy."

30. Responsibility—Young person accepts and takes personal responsibility.

31. Restraint—Young person believes it is important not to be sexually active or use alcohol or other drugs.

Social competencies

32. Planning and decision making—Young person knows how to plan ahead and make choices.

33. Interpersonal competence—Young person has empathy, sensitivity, and friendship skills.

34. Cultural competence—Young person has knowledge of and comfort with people of different cultural, racial and ethnic backgrounds.

35. Resistance skills—Young person can resist negative peer pressure and dangerous situations.

36. Peaceful conflict resolution—Young people seek to resolve conflict nonviolently.

Positive identity

37. Personal power—Young person feels he or she has control over "things that happens to me."

38. Self-esteem—Young person reports having high self-esteem.

39. Sense of purpose—Young person reports that "my life has a purpose."

40. Positive view of personal future—Young person is optimistic about her or his personal future.

The 40 Developmental Assets should not be seen as a "magic bullet" or panacea. What it can be is a piece of vital research that can change the life and trajectory of a young person. It is important to say that missing assets can be attained through hard work—not just by the mentor but the young person's family, community, school and congregation. The successful mentor will find ways to involve as many positive asset-builders as possible. Mentoring can never be delivered in isolation.

Questions To Ponder

1. What assets do you feel you can help your mentee acquire?

2. Can you name three assets you wish you had while growing up?

3. What three concrete things can your mentoring program do to increase asset-building beyond one-to-one mentoring?

MENTOR'S SPIRITUAL REFLECTION
THE SEVEN HABITS OF HIGHLY EFFECTIVE FATHERS

Habit # 1

Let Your Presence Be Your Present. How can you strive to be in God's presence, yet refuse to be in your child's presence? You have to be there (I know you have to work). You can't buy your children's love and affection as a substitute for having access to you. Give love by sharing love. A roof, a filled fridge, clothes on the back is not good enough - that's part of the basic and expected family contract. Are you too busy playing golf, shining up your ride, going to lodge meeting, or mowing the lawn to spend quality time with your child/children? Do something with your family on a regular basis and I don't mean just going to church.

Habit # 2

Let Your Word be Your Bond. If you say it then do it. If you promised something then carry it out. Young people are learning about life from you. What are they seeing? What are they hearing? What are they feeling? Your word must mean something.

Fathers cannot afford to be tuned out because one day you will have to say something important, something that could save your child's life and you want to be believed, heard and respected.

Habit # 3

Fight The Real Family Enemy The enemy is not your spouse. The enemy is not your children. I am tired of seeing people who use their children like pawns in some personal marital chess game. The real enemy seeks to kill, rob and destroy you and your family. The enemy you should be fighting is low self-esteem, low aspirations, drugs, depression, crime, gangs, low or non-functioning schools (prison is the graduate school of failing schools). Know that the weapons of our warfare are not carnal.

Habit # 4

Be a Giver and Not a Taker A father that is selfish and cannot see beyond his own needs or satisfying his own wants should relinquish the title of father. I remember hearing about a man that came home late with a chicken box for dinner. He knew his wife and daughter did not eat. He sat down in front of them and ate all of the chicken, not offering a morsel to his family. This man was a clueless taker. Sharing was an alien concept to him.

Habit # 5

Please Watch Your Step It is a fact that one step can take you closer to God or closer to the enemy and your whole family will be impacted depending on your choice. So you must watch where you are stepping. That means no sidestepping your responsibilities even when circumstances are tough. No stepping in and out of the church depending on your mood, who is preaching or according to any other "man" idiosyncrasies only deciphered by you. No stepping out with other women in or out of the church. Strive to step toward the light, not alone mind you, but leading your whole family.

Habit # 6

Have a Vision for You and Your Family. What do you want for your family? What is it that you are willing to sacrifice your all to attain? Is it for new suits, shoes, shirts and ties all for you? Is it a new lawnmower; or a new car? Too many fathers have grown content chasing dreams but never make time or worse, see the need to develop a vision for themselves or family. What is your operating vision that takes you and your family to the desired next level? Remember having a vision is nice but working hard to make the vision come true is the best.

Habit # 7

Pray, Praise and Worship God at Home. Do you praise the Lord at home with your family? Has your child, your spouse, other family members seen you caught up in the Spirit in your living room or den? Do you pray with your children (not just for your children)? Some men may say no to some or all of these questions. Perhaps their father never prayed with them. If so, YOU can start anew. Fathers, you do not have to be a hostage to the past. You can do a new thing that benefits you as a man of God and benefit your family. Men it is ALRIGHT to pray, praise and worship the Lord in your home.

There you have it, Seven Habits that move you toward being the best father possible to your children. Now go forth, you are authorized to practice and share The

Seven Habits of Highly Effective Fathers with men and young fathers.

MENTOR'S TESTIMONY

By David Banks Esq., CEO of The Eagle Academy

David Banks is one of the foremost educators in America. He left a budding career as a lawyer in the New York State Attorney General's Office to go back to school to get a Master's Degree to become a principal. David Banks' epitomizes what assets can do when richly bestowed on a child by family, community, school and church. David Banks dad, Phil Banks Jr. is the past President of 100 Black Men. This august group had the vision to start an all-male public school in New York City. The Eagle Academy, started in The South Bronx, is now in Brooklyn, Southeast Queens and a school is slated to open in Newark, NJ. The Eagle Academy ethos is to help young boys of color to soar above mediocrity and fly toward their destiny. Every student in the school has a mentor. David Banks' response is to an email I sent out to several prominent brothers about a moment that changed their life.

After reading your letter about offering a moment that changed my life and can also be applied to the young people we work with, I must mention growing up on 223rd Street between 116th Avenue and 115th Street in Cambria

Heights Queens, in the City of New York! That block was an "Oasis" because the parents of all the sixty plus families guided and inspired me to be the best young man I could be. I was saturated with knowledge nuggets that taught lessons of being culturally conscious and always helping one another as much as we could. I grew into a young man believing I could become anything I worked and strived to become as long as I always remembered to give back to my community to make things better than when I arrived!

My two younger brothers and I had our initial growing pains in Brooklyn with my mom and dad. We moved out of Brooklyn and came to Cambria Heights, on a street of families that were buying homes and guiding their children to a new part of life as owners of a piece of The Big Apple. I was thrilled with our new environment and meeting the other families on the block like the Sherwoods, the Lowes, the Rauses, and Dopson family to mention a few. They gave me the notion that excelling in education was the key to opening doors and making all of my dreams come true. I must admit that I was a pretty centered young man and was always a top student in my class because I really enjoyed going to school and was very inquisitive about learning things new and imaginative. My desire to make a difference in the world was a result of all of the positive advice I received from my family and neighbors.

I also observed the moves of many of the adults organizing and making our block beautiful, clean, and safe.

It kept me on point to make sure I presented my mother with a college degree for all the work she and my dad put in raising my brothers and me. My life today represents a compilation of all the advice, guidance, and inspiration I received. Other folk saw my potential as leader before I even knew I had the capacity. Growing up in Brooklyn taught me how to defend myself and to be aware of what was going on around me. The Queens experience residing in a home showed me how a consistent work ethic can get the things you need and want allowing your family to grow up in a positive environment with others who seek to be the best they can be!

Today, I'm the President/CEO of the Eagle Academy Foundation and this position is a result of more than two decades of work as a teacher, administrator, and principal in New York City Public schools. Even as I taught students from backgrounds similar to the Scholars in the Network of Eagle Academy Schools, I attended St. John's University Law School in the evenings. I thought I wanted to become a big time lawyer and represent families from the neighborhoods I grew up in. However, after completing Law School and working for the New York State Attorney General's Office, the love I had for teaching inspired me to go back to graduate school and get my certification to become a Principal and Administrator in the New York City Public School System. So, going into life thinking you're going to go into a specific career can change based on what you really love to do.

Now, I'm helping to save lives of young men and that's exactly what I want to do for the rest of my life. The work is hard because interaction with young men from sixth through twelfth grade is a tough business that most people don't want to get involved with. I'm very happy to be in the space God has chosen and my work is guided by the desire to help our young men always remember to give back to their communities. I want the thousands of young men to deliver a college degree to their mothers and fathers just like I did for all the love and guidance their parents gave. The young guys and girls I grew up with on 223rd Street have grown up to be a Police Chief in New York City, top educational administrators in Westchester and Nassau Counties, medical doctors, lawyers, business owners, Transit Authority supervisors, ranking police officers, and many other careers they are using to make New York City and the communities they reside in better than when they arrived. To God Be The Glory!

In the Interest of Excellence In Education...

CHAPTER FIVE

MENTOR'S "BE" TOOLS

*...be steadfast, immoveable, always abounding in the work
of the Lord, knowing that your labor is not in vain in the
Lord. 1Corinthians 15:58b (NKJV)*

One of the worst mentoring assumptions that can be made is that any man can be a mentor. This erroneous thought is exacerbated given the reality that it is hard to find men interested in becoming a mentor. There are both visible and invisible moving parts that make for a successful mentoring relationship and program. While the focus of mentoring should be on young people - it would be unwise not to look at what the mentor brings to the table. Here are some important mentor "Be" tools that can be helpful to ascertain if you are a good mentoring candidate and also evaluate mentor performance.

- *Be Consistent*—It is better not to mentor if you have trouble consistently sustaining the relationship due to not showing up. You cannot mentor when you feel like it or disappear when you get too busy or worse, don't feel like being bothered.

- *Be Responsible*—If you say it do it. Never get in the habit of not keeping your word. Always remember that your mentee may have experienced broken promises in the past so no need of you being another promise breaker. Mentees should be focused on what you do and not solely on what you say. Back in the day it was said, 'Talk is cheap.' It still is…

- **Be Caring**—If a young person knows that you care about them as a person he will allow you access into his inner domain. There are men that have a difficult time expressing compassion and therefore become content showing it rather than sharing it. That will not go far if it is the primary mode of intervention

- **Be Real**—Please don't invent a more dynamic or hardcore past in a vain attempt to help you relate to your mentee. If you make up a life you can't change a life. It is far easier to be yourself than constantly having to remember a reinvented self.

- **Be Flexible**—This does not mean be weak. Know when to bend when bending is helpful. It is important to note the difference between bending rules and ignoring rules. The benefit of a flexible approach is that it gives options in the form of varied opportunities to reach, teach and guide.

- *Be Patient*—Don't be quick to jump to hasty conclusions by giving advice before you know the full story or condemn after you heard part of the story. First listen, then reflect, then react. If patience is a virtue, unfortunately, some men are virtue less. Men are taught to be active and insert themselves into problems and SOLVE them. Waiting may seem like a big waste of time

- *Be Decisive*—There are thoughts, words and deeds that are not negotiable so don't make pledges of secrecy and be stuck with an issue that should be shared. For example if a child confides that he has suicidal thoughts, you should not make the decision that it is in the child's best interest to keep this troubling fact a secret until you figure out what to do or who to tell.

- *Be Aware*—Take note of what is going on in the life of a young person, especially since your mentee, depending on his age, is on a physiological, social, spiritual, emotional and hormonal roller coaster. It helps to remember when you were young and what you felt at the time. While times have changed feelings are relatively consistent.

- *Be Creative*—Try different ways to reach your mentee. Perhaps a group trip to a sporting event or visit to the museum would work. Reading and sharing thoughts from an appropriate book could be enriching. Listening to music your mentee likes and watching films could open the door to deeper discussion beyond the typical question: 'so what was your day like?'

- *Be Mature*—Don't claim to be a man and play childish head games (that you always must win). A grown man that acts like a boy and is in a position of power is a danger to himself and others. A grown man that has not matured needs a mentor before he can successfully be a mentor.

- *Be Reflective*—Think about what to say before you say it. If you hear something that runs counter to your sensibilities try your best not to be punitively reactive. A misspoken word can cancel out months and months of hard work. An errant thought can create an irreparable divide. A raised eyebrow signifying judgment or skepticism can stop a conversation dead in its tracks

- *Be Competent*—It is important to avail yourself for mentor training learning adolescent and youth development. It is good for a man to have a desire to work with youth but it is great to have desire and demonstrated competency.

- *Be Multidimensional*—Allow the full spectrum of your various interests and personality to show. There are times to be serious and there are times to have fun. Please pray to know the difference. If you work with young people and don't like to have fun you are in the wrong business. On the other end of the spectrum don't forget to show your thoughtful side and share lessons you had to learn in order to become who you are.

- *Be Confident*—You must believe that you have the ability, tenacity and spirit to make a difference in the life of your mentee. Your unwavering belief that change is possible is the fuel a young person may need to travel beyond the barrier of what is known and dissatisfying to what is unknown and potentially fulfilling.

- *Be Prayerful*—Unlike secular programs it is alright to pray with and for your mentee and his family. Please don't forget to pray for yourself and your family. A praying man is a "dangerous" man. A praying man can speak things into existence. A praying man can loose and bind by the power of the Holy Spirit.

I am not handy with tools. My wife jokes that if a household problem can't be fixed by a screwdriver then it won't be fixed by me. Men, we must not have a 'screwdriver only approach' to mentoring in an attempt to solving a staggering array of problems. We need to be adept at using all of the "B" Tools in our toolkit to reach young people where they are and where they hurt. And for master craftsmen, it is important to teach what you know to apprentices.

Questions to Ponder

1. What other "B" Tools can you recommend that a mentor possess in order to be effective?

2. What "B" Tool on the list is easiest for you to present and which one is more difficult for you to present?

3. What "B" Tools were helpful in reaching you when you needed help? Bonus "B" question: What "B" tool was missing in your growing up?

MENTOR'S SPIRITUAL REFLECTION
LOOKING FOR A FEW GOOD MEN
Matthew 28:16-20

Ralph Ellison, the distinguished African-American author's greatest work was *The Invisible Man.* Ellison's breath-taking novel was written during the Harlem Renaissance. The book stated that the needs, pains, hopes, dreams, aspirations, contributions, strength and resilience of black men in America were unimportant. Null and void. In essence, black men were invisible to mainstream America and the world. This word is issued as a challenge to today's invisible men who refuse to be heard from, opt not to be known, dwell in shadows; men who don't want to be touched or wished to be seen. The Lord is looking for a few good men! It is time for men to live out God's plan for your life. It is time to look at The Great Commission, not as something that only the disciples were tasked to heed, but as something that every believing man must do!

The United States Marine Corp's recruitment campaign states that they are looking for a few good men. I've got news for The Marines; Jesus beat them to it by over 2,000 years. The Lord was looking for a few good men while He walked the earth. Jesus is still looking for a few good men to fight a timeless battle between good and evil. Men, you are Jesus' eyes, His hands, and His feet. You are His emissaries charged with going into a world that is rife with hate, self-centeredness, violence, oppression, lust and greed. If you render yourself invisible then the transformative power of Jesus becomes invisible to others. If you don't tell that young brother that you were once blind, but now you see who will? That you were once broken but have been made whole. That you were once down but you got back up because of Jesus in your life. It is imperative that you share how you got from there to here. Young people need to know it is possible to transcend one's circumstance. Let your mentee know it is not where you start out in life that is important but it is where you end up that counts.

African-Americans come from an historic line of good men who firmly believed that the whole can be greater than the sum of its parts. Some of the names of illustrious men that not only made history but also changed history are: Denmark Vesey, Toussaint L'Ouverture, Nat Turner, Richard Allen, Frederick Douglass, W.E.B. Du Bois, Booker T. Washington, Dr. Charles Drew, Langston Hughes, Malcolm X, Martin Luther King and most recently, President Barack Hussein Obama.

I truly admire what these giants were able to do under the most taxing circumstances. They should get their props; but what about the good men who were invisible to the scribes of history? What about those nameless faceless men in the Bible? Is their testimony relevant to today's man? Let's go to the text and see what helpful and potentially transformative message invisible men can tell us.

You remember the paralytic man who lay by the pool for 38 years? This nameless man wants you to know that if you are to live out God's purpose for your life you have to want to be made well. Put down your favorite excuses even the ones that you really believe. Then Get Up. Pick Up. Stand Up on your own two feet (John 5:1-8). Another man in the Bible identified by his condition was the leper who was fortunate to be in the right place at the right time (Luke 17:11-19). Ten lepers were cleansed of their disease but only one came back to Jesus to say thank you. The Bible tells us that the leprous man fell down at Jesus' feet and in a loud voice thanked and worshiped Him. Only if men would worship The Lord! Do you have anything to worship Him for? Has he healed you? Restored you?

But wait a minute let's get closer to home. There were men in our lives, men in our family lineage who are not recorded in the history books. Yet these men were chosen by God for a mighty work. They were janitors, sharecroppers, self-taught preachers; they were Pullman porters on trains. Mainstream America did not know that these invisible men were fathers, husbands, providers, churchmen. What about your father, your grandfather or your great grandfather? Many of these men did not have formal education or seemingly did not have much to look forward to in life. They were lynched with impunity. They were sharecropped to death. They were 'buked and scorned.' Jim Crow laws reinforced by the Supreme Court made separate but equal (unequal) the law of the land. Our elders were ridiculed in all forms of existing media. One of the earliest films shown in America was *Birth Of A Nation*. This film drew on the racist threads deeply woven in America's psyche showing the awesome power of media to negatively define sons and daughters of slaves.

Some of the men who were vilified and negatively caricatured by hate-filled Southerners and Northerners willpower may have given out but the spirit of these strong men would never quit. My grandfather, a lifelong deacon of Mt. Pleasant Baptist Church, lived on 137th Street right off of Lenox Avenue in Harlem from the mid 1920's until his death in 1978. He was a veteran of World War I. When he came back from overseas, he wasn't referred to as Mr. Roland Allison outside of Harlem. He was looked upon as the boy who ran the elevator in a downtown office building. He was by all accounts a nameless, faceless invisible man to society. He may have been nobody on Tuesday. His shoulders may have drooped a little on Wednesday. He may have cried on Thursday. But he knew if he could just get to the temple on Sunday that everything would be alright. When Sunday came our fathers, grandfathers, great grandfathers, and men unknown to us shook off the insults of the world and got dressed up and headed to worship services.

They did not stumble into church. They did not shuffle to their seats. These men, chosen by God, did not look down at their feet. No, they marched, they strutted, they hooped and hollered. They may have been called Tom, Boy, George, Shine, Uncle, Coon in the street but when they stepped into the church, when they got to the sanctuary, they shed the world's definition and took on God's definition, namely, fearfully and wonderfully made. They were the few good men chosen by God. In church they were known as sir, mister, usher, deacon, trustee, brother or Pastor. These men who were invisible in the world were made visible in the sight of God.

They had no problem praising the Lord. They took every opportunity to lift Holy hands toward heaven. They had to refill their spiritual tanks to deal with the Hell they would catch on Monday. They were the few good men who refused to be defined by the world's standards or marginalized by racism! These brothers were the few good men who raised families; sent sons and daughters off to college.

I am talking about the few good men who refused to be broken or rendered invisible to their community, family or church. Through their sacrifices; through their pains; through their tears; and sustained through prayer, they knew they could not give up. They refused to be nobodies because they knew deep in their souls they had been anointed and appointed by God.

The Lord is still looking for a few good men that fit the following criteria:

> Deal with their inner issues and refuse to live with hurt/pain.
>
> Be responsible mentors worth following.
>
> Reconcile to be the best sons, fathers, providers and friends.
>
> Love themselves and can show tender/faithful love to others.
>
> Not ashamed of the Gospel of Jesus Christ.
>
> Praise the Lord in season and out - and in the home with family.
>
> Will not ego trip on who they are, what they drive, or what they have.

> Be a faithful and trustworthy servant in and out of church.
>
> Be role models to mentee, peers, family and community.
>
> Visit the sick, clothe the naked and feed the hungry.
>
> Know that women are not their enemy or to be used as sport.
>
> Won't be a domestic terrorist to their families.
>
> Will go out of the church and bring folk into the church.
>
> Will love God with their whole heart, mind and soul.

Are you that man? Are you the one that the Lord wants to send out to mentor a young brother being recruited by gangs or just leaving prison? Are you the one who will help a young man exiting a drug treatment program adjust to life living clean and sober? Do you feel a tug in your spirit to help boys in juvenile detention facilities or keep the young brothers on the street from going in? Can you help a brother learn how to be a father? Can you help a sister doing her best to raise her son without helping yourself? Do you feel that you can and must do more; in short be a brother to a brother? If this is you, know that you are one of the few good men being called to carry out a 21st Century style Great Commission. Here is your mandate:

"All authority in heaven and on earth has been given to me. Therefore go and make disciples of all nations, baptizing them in the name of the Father, Son and Holy Spirit, and teaching them to obey everything I commanded you. And surely I am with you always, to the very end of the age." Matthew 28:18b-20

MENTOR'S MISSION FUEL
ROADBLOCKS, HAZARDS AND DETOURS FOR MEN ON DESTINY'S ROAD

Paul was the quintessential communicator. He was able to hang with the Greek philosophers; the Roman mystics, the pious Jews and was even able to speak Aramaic (Hebrew dialect used by common folk and Jesus). One of Paul's special gifts was using metaphors to explain spiritual truths. A consistent allusion he used dealt with sports. For example, he told The Ephesians, "We wrestle not against flesh and blood (6:12a NKJV). He told The Philippians, "I press on toward the goal to win the prize (marathoner's victory wreath) of the high calling… (Phil 3:14). He told Timothy near the end of his life, I have fought the good fight, I have finished the race (2Tim 4:7).

I will borrow a technique from Paul and use a teaching metaphor that men can relate to and that is a car. Think, you are in a car and your destiny is somewhere down life's road. You will never meet your destiny if you decide (free-will) to sit in your parked vehicle; if you are blocked in; or if you are headed in the wrong direction. If you do decide to head toward your destiny, your adversary will put up roadblocks, hazards and detours along the way. This is all done to get men to abort their journey, get lost, breakdown, or, most desired, die in an 'accident.'

Today's automobiles have more computing power than what existed in the Apollo rockets that took astronauts to the Moon. The car's computer can be hooked up to a diagnostic machine and the internal functions can be analyzed. One of the sure signs that something is amiss is the amber Check Engine light that we all have ignored some time during our driving experience. So here is a report that can be sent in about all of us before we take to the road:

DIAGNOSTIC TUNE UP RESULT

The good that I would do I do not. And that what I should not do that is what I do... Romans 7:15a

Road Signs

1. **Yield To Oncoming Traffic**—It is hard for men to yield. It implies submission. Men are trained from birth not to submit. Submission is encased in macho theory and in a man's world is always looked upon as weakness. It has been said on the playing field:

quitters never win and winners never quit (hear submit).

2. **Rough Road Ahead**—There are times in life when it is important to slow down due to hazardous road surface. We all will have bumpy roads to travel from time-to-time. Have you ever hit a pothole that shook or damaged your vehicle because you were traveling too fast? Watch out for life's potholes. They are hidden from easy view (but can be seen). Potholes, depending on the size, can be dangerous to you and your vehicle.

3. **Speed Limit Posting**—Some men like to drive fast to get to their destination quicker. What if you are speeding and don't know where you are going or run into another vehicle? It has been proven by experts that drivers tend to speed up in foggy conditions. Is that your driving testimony? Sometimes you will be pulled over for speeding. It is not punishment; it can save your life.

4. **Stop Sign**—It is easy to run a stop sign especially when one's attention wanders. Stop signs are placed strategically to slow you down so you do not venture out in a busy intersection. It is possible to run life's stop sign and nothing happens (lucky). A

driver should NEVER consistently place their life in luck's hands.

5. <u>Gas</u>—In order to run your engine you must have fuel. Some drivers (not my wife) wait until the fuel light come on and you still drive past gas stations. The danger (and game) is thinking you can make it to your destination before running out of gas. You drive with one eye on the road and the other eye on the light. This is self-induced anxiety and frustration that does not have to be.

6. <u>Repair Shop</u>—It is important to do preventive maintenance work so your vehicle can be in peak operating condition. Some drivers will not go into the shop until it is too late. It is the same mentality that keeps men from going to the doctor. This is doubly sad when preventive maintenance could have forestalled a complete breakdown (heart attack/stroke/cancer).

7. <u>Tow Away Zone</u>—There are some places you cannot park. If this sign is not obeyed your vehicle can be taken away from you and redeemed only after paying a hefty sum. No driver wants to be towed. Most who park illegally think: I will be back before the tow truck; or think that it is other people that get towed - or they totally misread the sign.

8. **Rest Stop Ahead**—It is important to get rest especially on long trips. You cannot drive effectively if you are too tired to keep your eyes open. Yet some drivers feel strong enough to push pass their fatigue. They feel they have another driving gear. Better to arrive at your destination safe and in one piece than not arrive at all.

ROAD TIPS THAT CAN SAVE YOUR LIFE

- A good driver always uses his signal indicator to alert other drivers he is about to merge or make a turn. On destiny's road there are many exits and turns - some visible and predictable and others not. It is easier to signal when you know where you are going.

- Sometimes the driver will have to use his flashers to warn other vehicles of a hazard. It would be a mistake to believe that the unseen hazard can be negotiated by you and therefore there is no need to slow down because of your superior driving skills. Or the fact you are always in a hurry and drive aggressively all the time. For all you know the first driver could be flashing because he is at a train crossing or the bridge is washed out ahead.

- Always have your rear view mirror properly adjusted so you can view what is behind you as you move forward. There are people, places and things that should remain in your rear view mirror. You cannot drive forward and constantly look backward.

- Don't race your engine in the red zone posted on your tachometer. Just because it can go there does not mean it can stay there!

- When traveling through unknown areas of life use GPS (God Positioning Souls) so you can be guided to your destination. You may know where you want to end up but don't know how to get there. Your supernatural GPS will lead you past the cross in the road so you can find your destined destination.

You may find in the course of your life travels that you may be headed in the wrong direction. Perhaps you will find yourself headed down the wrong road for a short or long period of time depending on your sense of direction or your inclination not to ask for directions. It does not matter. There will come a time that you are clear and say to self or to others (some may have been warning you that you were headed down the wrong road) that I am lost. I missed a turn, a merge point, an exit or something. It is at this point that you exercise the supreme driving maneuver that allows you to turnaround and move in the opposite direction. It is called a U-turn. Some U-turns are done in three precise moves. Other U-turns are executed in a slow unsure manner. Then there are drivers that have to go around several corners before heading in the right direction. This tells us that drivers headed in the wrong direction, prayerfully, will find various ways to make a U-turn.

Let's look at U-turns some brothers have made or need to make:

- You turn from habits, people, places and things that no longer define you. You turn out of darkness into the glorious light.
- You turn from being a deadbeat father and take care of your children. You turn from always making excuses that keep you immobilized.
- You turn from your problems and surrender your all to the Divine problem-solver.

Look over to the right. There is your exit. You wonder how you missed it so many times. Your GPS tells you that you are on Revelation Highway and that you are headed toward Abundant Joy Way. You don't know how long it will take to get to your final destination which is Pearly Gates off of The King's Highway but you contently drive knowing you are finally headed in the right direction.

Questions to Ponder

1. What hazards that could have ruined your trip down Destiny Road have you encountered and/or manage to avoid?

2. What detours have you taken and where did you end up?

3. What three things are you happy to say are in your rear view mirror?

MENTORS TESTIMONY
THE POWER OF RELATIONSHIPS
By Stanley Brown

Stanley Brown, Head of A&R RCA/Sony Inspirational, is an award winning, multiplatinum, Musician, Producer and Composer with over twenty years of experience in the music industry working in: advertising, television, film and with a diverse list of recording artist. He possesses both a musical ear and strong business sense that has allowed him to excel. Stanley Brown has worked with The Temptations, India.Arie, Run DMC, Donald Lawrence, Dru Hill, Hezekiah Walker,

Keith Sweat, T.D. Jakes, Bell Biv Devoe, Will Downing, Vickee Winans, Salt-n-Pepa, Karen Clarke-Sheard, Guy, Marvin Sapp, Christopher Williams and Bobby Brown to name a few. He has served as Vice President of A&R for Island Black Music and Senior Director of A&R for Motown Records. Currently, Stanley Brown is Senior Director of A&R for Verity Gospel Music Group, a subsidiary of Sony Music Entertainment and President/CEO of Timeless Music Group. Some clients include: Universal Music Group, General Motors, McDonalds, Walmart, Verizon Wireless, Subway and The BET Network. Stanley Brown also serves as Music Director for The Greater Allen A.M.E. Cathedral of New York and was Music Director for BET's gospel music competition show, Sunday Best!

In 1997 I was working as a young A&R executive with Island Records. In my dealings, I met a man who was a world renowned boxing promoter and artist manager named Ronald "Butch" Lewis (Everyone called him Butch). He was considered big time to me and was someone I enjoyed doing business with at the time. He approached me about giving one of his Vegas acts a record deal with the label but she was not what we were in the market for so I had to decline. Through his persistence it wasn't long before I was able to work out a role for the artist on the film sound track of a Whoopie Goldberg movie called "Eddie." After sealing that deal for Butch's singer, he felt indebted to me because I helped him make good on his promise to his artist. As an act of kindness he would fly me to Las Vegas to enjoy major boxing matches. I would have great seats on the front row and I was sitting among dignitaries, celebrities, professional athletes and other people of prominence.

It wasn't long after when Island Records merged with Def Jam and the move left me unemployed. Butch generously offered me a job making $500 a week. That was a huge and humbling drop from the six-figure salary Island Records was paying me. With no other income stream, I took the job as an assistant to Butch. I had to see this as a step in the right direction as I was able to glean from the business savvy he possessed. I had a love for the music and entertainment industry and helping him was the only avenue that kept me connected. While I was gaining knowledge watching him work, he was also making calls on my behalf to help me get reestablished in the record industry. With my standard of living in free-fall, I was on the verge of losing a very comfortable lifestyle in Edgewater, NJ along the Hudson River.

There was an occasion while working for Butch when he called and asked me to drive him into Manhattan for a meeting with HBO. This was how I was earning my "just" above minimum wage salary. We had a conversation on that drive to HBO that forever changed my perspective on life's priorities. I picked up Butch at his apartment in my new Mercedes S 500 (One of the few luxuries I managed to hold on to). Sitting in the passenger seat and smoking a cigar, my boss tells me that he left his check book at his apartment. Not wanting to be late for the meeting he asked me to go to my bank and withdraw $75,000 for him to take to the meeting. He promised he would pay me back when we returned to his home. While I was confident he meant it; I had to confess saying, "I don't have that kind of money in the bank."

Hearing this, Butch tells me not to wait for him after I drop him off at HBO. He says to me, "Take the car back to the Mercedes dealer and let them know I am not grown enough for this car." I looked at him like he was out of his mind. He said, "You can't have $75,000 on the street and no money in the bank." I went to the Mercedes dealer and returned the car of my dreams. I spent a season depending on public transportation to get around. Those life-changing words have stuck in my head as if he said them yesterday. But that is what it was like working for Butch who would teach me many valuable business lessons. He would always tell me, "Stay in the trenches and you'll eventually have what you want out of life." He assured me that it was not going to be comfortable saying I'd have to step up my grind if I was to make something out of myself in the music business.

Doing those menial tasks and just getting by on a $500 a week salary, was well worth the wisdom I gained working for Butch. His mentorship helped steer me to the many achievements that would follow including a dream job with RCA/Sony Records. I work full-time in the music industry with leading secular and Gospel recording artists. I am grateful for every bump on my head that got me here. But I'm all the more grateful that my mentor cared and saw something in me worth the investment of his time and sharing his life experience.

CHAPTER SIX

MENTOR'S POWER TO EMPOWER

"I will give you the keys of the kingdom of heaven;
whatever you bind on earth shall be bound in heaven, and
whatever you loose on earth shall be loosed in heaven".
(Matthew 16:19)

In my travels around the country making speeches and delivering youth development training, I am frequently asked to do a workshop I created called The Power of One. This interactive experience is based on youth resiliency research that looked at young people from around the world growing up in very trying circumstances. The research shows that the two consistent factors that helped troubled young people rise above their circumstance were a sense of humor (making lemonade out of lemons) and a consistent and caring adult presence in their lives. Yes, one person has the power to make a difference in the life of another human being. On a trip to Portland, Oregon I asked this simple question: "How have you made a difference in the life of a young person?" I want to report this different and surprising response filtered through this scriptural reference and perspective: *Let the weak say they are strong.*

CLEAN COOKIES

After asking the question how you have made a difference in the life of a young person one of the women in my group reluctantly raised her hand in response. She was sitting next to her daughter and up to this point both seemed comfortable to be silent members of the workshop. She cleared her throat, seemingly unsure if her response was going to answer my question. She said that she had been a housewife for over 20 years. At the point that all of her children were out of the house, she decided to volunteer at the local high school her daughter attended.

After several weeks she began to question her decision. While she loved volunteering she was shocked by the rampant profanity used by the students. She felt like a modern day Rip Van Winkle waking up in a profane town. She decided that the end of the week would be the end of her volunteer stint. She felt bad about leaving but her feeling of helplessness in addressing the profanity in the classrooms, hallways and stairwells was overwhelming.

She decided her last "official" act would be to say good-bye by baking her family's favorite chocolate chip cookies. News about the cookies spread around the school. Soon, there was a long line of students waiting for cookies. The woman prayed a silent prayer and then said these words to the students that changed everything. "I must warn you that these are 'clean' cookies and if you eat them, they will clean up your language."

The young people laughed as they happily ate the cookies. Then the most amazing thing happened over the following days; if one of the young people cursed in her presence, they would excuse their language. She was energized by what she saw and soon began baking 'clean' pies and 'clean' cakes. Within weeks the cursing that was so prevalent in the school subsided to an almost nonexistent level. This volunteer who wanted to give up was credited with changing the culture of an entire institution with her 'clean' cookies.

I learned an important lesson from this testimony. The woman's power to curb the profanity did not come from her size, forcefulness, personality or cunning. Her earnest prayer, offered at a time of certain defeat, was for the right words to tell the young people that she was leaving the school. God's immediate response, on face value, did not seem to address the circumstance, but upon further review, truly made the ordinary extraordinary.

I know some of you may think just as Jesus turned water into wine, that He made a supernatural batch of chocolate chip clean cookies. Not so. The woman may have felt like a failure but she discovered the power in saying and then doing the right thing at the right time. Unfortunately, some mentors and parents have become accustomed to saying the right thing at the wrong time or worse, saying the wrong thing at the right time. From that day forward our spirit-filled baker knew that the weak can become strong - not by power, not by might but by the Lord's spirit (and blessed 'clean' cookies!).

Questions To Ponder

1. If you could talk to a person or persons that made a difference in your life who would you call and what would you say?

2. Have you ever helped a person who was at a critical point of need? What was the circumstance; what did you do and how did it make you feel?

3. Have you ever been in a position where you felt overmatched in addressing a particular issue but in the end you were able to get the victory? If so please give the circumstance.

MENTOR'S SPIRITUAL REFLECTION
MEN IT'S TIME TO COME CLEAN
2 Kings 5:1-16

This story is about a man named Naaman. He had a serious problem. This man by scriptural account was a macho man. He was strong, brave and independent. Naaman was a man's man who had what so many men crave namely: position, power and prestige. And with all of his success, with all of his connections, with all of his money, Naaman had to face the fact that while things seemed perfect on the outside, he had an issue that ate away at his joy; something that stole his peace of mind. He had a problem that was keeping him up at night. Naaman was smitten with leprosy. Leprosy literally caused one's limbs to fester, ooze, rot and eventually fall away from the bone. If you were a leper in that day, you had to move away from your family and friends and live as an outcast in leper caves. In Jewish tradition if anyone came near the leper had to yell this warning, "Unclean." "Unclean."

You can imagine Naaman's fear. He had to wonder, how will my family manage when I die? What about all of my hopes and dreams? How long will I live? Will I die alone? The Bible tells us that a servant girl of Naaman told his wife that if only her husband could see the great prophet Elisha in Samaria then he would be healed. Ms. Naaman obviously loved her husband and was probably also at her wits end. She immediately told Naaman what the servant girl said. Naaman went to the King saying, 'I've got to get to Israel and I need your help.' So the King wrote a letter to the King of Israel stating that he must heal Naaman of his leprosy.

When the King of Israel read the letter, the Bible tells us that he became vexed in his spirit. He asked, "Am I God, can I kill and bring someone back to life?" The King knew his limitations. He was wise enough to know that while he had great power, he did not have power to heal the sick, to set sin's captives free, or cure leprosy. The Word tells us that Elisha heard that the mighty King of Israel tore his clothing in sorrow and also out of fear (he thought he was being set-up). Elisha sent word to the King to have Naaman come to see him.

My brothers, if we would only trust God and not our macho drenched maleness, virility, or male privilege we will experience the true move of God's power in our lives. This is hard to do because trusting self is what we are conditioned to do. Naaman took riches to the man of God because he thought he had to buy a blessing. So many brothers worship materialism: what they wear, where they live or what they drive. Can your clothes heal you? Can your house comfort you? Can your looks counsel you? As Naaman neared the prophet's home, he was informed by Elisha's servant that he should go and wash himself seven times in the Jordan and he would be cleansed. Naaman became angry. His macho spirit flamed out of control. Naaman fumed when he heard from a lowly messenger and not the prophet. Naaman was about to make a mistake that many men are still guilty of making. He was about to abort his blessing. He almost allowed his manly pride to get in the way of his healing. Naaman dismissively asked, "Are not Abana and Pharpar, the rivers of Damascus better than any of the waters of Israel? Couldn't I wash in them and be cleansed?"

Roughly translated Naaman was saying, 'I didn't come all the way over here to dip myself in this mud hole! I will not be insulted by another man who does not have what I have. He doesn't drive what I drive. He doesn't command any troops. This insolent prophet does not have the decency or sense of respect to see me, Naaman, face-to-face, man-to-man.' Just like Naaman, there are many brothers who are hurt, confused desperate or so angry they lash out at anyone who is close to them: their spouse, children, people on the job, folk in the church. They are angry at a daddy who either was too mean, too distant or was never there for them. These brothers have unresolved issues that are festering like the leprosy on Naaman's body. They want relief. They want to be healed. They want to be made clean.

There are so many boys and men who have grown up without a strong, consistent and caring man in their lives. These brothers carry their hurts through life. While we may not have leprosy like Naaman, we have other afflictions like past wrongs that are hijacking our future by haunting our present. One of Naaman's servants spoke boldly to his master, saying, "My father, if the prophet told you to do some great thing, would you not have done it?" The servant basically said what have you got to lose? What are you giving up? Naaman swallowed his pride and dipped into the Jordan seven times as instructed and his flesh became clean like that of a young boy. Naaman got his healing. He got his breakthrough. He was delivered. He was clean.

Men this should remind all of us that there will come a time when you have to face your fears, problems, your inner mess; confront your issues that you don't want people to know are still inside of you. I am talking about that secret sin, boiling anger and hidden fear. Fear that you are not who you say you are. Fear that you don't quite measure up. Fear that you are not as manly as you wish or others think.

My brothers it's time to come clean. It is time to deal with your personal leprosy that is slowly eating away at your mind, heart, soul and future. You may be a 'church hopper', a pew sitter, a deacon, trustee, usher, a choir member, liturgical dancer, praise leader or preacher. You may be old or young, light or dark, tall or short, thin or fat, rich or poor, it does not matter. I've got good news, your release is nigh. Your healing is here. Just like Naaman, it is time for you to come clean! It is time to confront what is causing you to live beneath your privilege or out of the perfect will of God. You don't have to dip in the Jordan seven times. You don't have to journey to meet a prophet.

Your day of deliverance is now. It is time to come clean. When you are clean, you can let go of that bad attitude. You can let go of pain; hurt; disappointment; depression; and living nightmares. It is time to come clean. You have been dragging your 'man mess" through life far too long. It is time to let go and truly let God. You see the cleaned up man is born again in the very image of Christ. The cleaned up man can forgive. The cleaned up man does not always have to have his own way – all the time. The cleaned up man is never violent or threatening to his spouse, children or friends. The cleaned up man does not front like a saint in church and a hellion in the street. The cleaned up man handles his business; he is responsible and wants to grow in wisdom and grace.

If there are some men who want a clean break and lasting change in their heart, mind and soul, I want you to know that Jesus has some living water that will clean you. Come on brothers take a sip. It's time to come clean.

Questions to Ponder

1. What hit you hardest when you read the account of Naaman?

2. Can you remember a time (or times) that your pride got in the way of a blessing for you?

3. If you could dip in the Jordan like Naaman what would you like to rid yourself of and thus become clean?

MENTOR'S MISSION FUEL
LITTLE CAN BECOME MUCH

I taught a class for several years at New York Theological Seminary titled Urban Youth and Theology. I asked the Power of One question and each student in the class had to respond. The stories were like a mini-sermon on how ordinary people can make an extraordinary difference in the life of another person. By the time we went around the room, we laughed, expressed wonder, but mainly cried as we saw God's hand moving on the heart of people to help others at a vulnerable time in life.

My co-leader colleague and friend, the Rev Dr. C. Vernon Mason, recalled how a poor man from his town (where he 'chopped' cotton to make ends meet) gave him $38.00 so he could pay the registration fee after being accepted to Morehouse College. Up to this point he did not know where the money would come from. The money had to be turned in by a fast approaching deadline or the acceptance offer would be withdrawn. A love deposit of $38.00 was given by a man who also chopped cotton in the same town where Bro. Mason grew up. His sacrificial gift of $38.00 changed young Mason's life.

Today, Dr. C. Vernon Mason holds a B.A. J.D., MBA, M.Div. and D. Min. Dr. Mason became a prominent civil rights attorney; a former visiting seminary professor, a champion of court adjudicated youth and was ordained in one of the leading churches in America. I have heard this story several times and each time it is told Dr. Mason tears up like it just happened yesterday. I believe his tears are mixed with gratefulness and the thought what would his life be like if he was not given the $38.00 to register for college.

Brothers you must believe that you have power to change another person's life. This power is not from you but comes through you. Please know that there is a big difference between thinking you may have power and knowing that you have access to life-changing power. If you still are not sure about the power of one think back to a difference maker in your life.

MENTOR'S TESTIMONY
THE RENAISSANCE MAN
By Marvin Pierre

A friend teaching in an inner-city public school asked Marvin to come to his troubled school as a career day presenter. He was so appalled by the students' lack of reading skills and despair, he soon left his well-paying private sector job at a leading New York City investment bank and went into the public school system. Bro. Pierre is now dean of students at a charter school. He is a member of The Greater Allen Cathedral of New York and founder of Sons of Promise, a mentoring program for boys between the ages of 8-12. Bro. Pierre graduated from Trinity College.

I am currently the Dean of Students of an all-boys school in Bedford-Stuyvesant Brooklyn, NY. Every morning I greet 400 boys, as they enter our school building. For every handshake, I ask myself, will this young man make it to college and beyond? This is the same question that many of my school teachers asked about me growing up in the impoverished community of South Jamaica Queens, NY. I was a young boy that lacked direction and needed immediate intervention. The turning point in my life came when my Pop Warner football coach, sent me to a prominent boarding school in Cape Cod, Massachusetts, called Tabor Academy.

My experience at Tabor Academy was life changing. It was there that I met my surrogate father and mentor Dr. Samuel McFadden. He was a Radiologist at Toby Hospital in Wareham, Massachusetts, with a commitment to humanity. His involvement in my life put me on a path for achievement, changing my life completely. Dr. McFadden understood the necessity of boys having role models, structure, and a realization of potential. He constantly reminded me to surround myself with the right people. He had this one saying, "If you surround yourself with people that are going places, they'll take you with them."

Today, in my role as Dean of Students, I have an opportunity to guide the next generation of leaders. Although, I am successful in this role, if it had not been for the lasting influence that Dr. McFadden had on my life, I wouldn't be doing this work. Similar to Dr. McFadden's role in my life, I now play the role of a surrogate father and mentor to a twelve-year old boy name K. J (initials only). I began my relationship with him when he was ten years old. He came from a family that provided him with very little structure, accountability and most important, love. This harsh reality is very common for young boys who lack guidance and support.

My successful impact in K.J.'s life was the motivation behind starting my mentoring and empowerment program for Black and Latino boys called **"Sons of Promise."** I realized that the work I was doing to change his life could be replicated with the right vision and action plan. In Spring 2009, I stepped out on faith and officially launched **"Sons of Promise."** As the founder of the program, it was my desire to expose black boys from the inner-city to more positive male role models, similar to my personal experience at Tabor Academy. Our mission is to provide middle school males with relevant experiences that would ensure their success academically, socially, and professionally. These young boys learn about the importance of Manhood, Scholarship, Perseverance, and Brotherhood.

Overall, as an active advocate for black and Latino boys in this country, I message to every young boy that I mentor, that each one of them has the potential to achieve anything they want in life. They were born with many talents that they don't even know they have. I challenge them to learn from their mistakes and the mistakes of others. I strive to keep them persistent and accept disappointments and failures as a learning experience on the road to success. They are defined by what you stand for and I remind them that their integrity is not for sale.

I don't know what the future holds for me in regards to my role with youth, but each morning that I wake up, I thank God for the ability to make a difference in the lives of young boys.

CHAPTER SEVEN

MENTOR'S PROMISE SEEDS

"... Still other seed fell on good soil. It came up and yielded a crop a hundred times more than was sown... "
Luke 8:8

I t has been said that from a small acorn seed springs forth the mighty oak. Words can be much like seeds if planted at the right time, place, and if properly attended, something great can spring forth. A mentor is like a farmer planting seeds of hope, inner-direction and elevation in their young charge. Any farmer worth his salt will never plant a seed then turn around and doubt if anything will grow. A farmer, dependent upon the crop for his and his family's sustenance, cannot afford to be a pessimist.

As a mentor, you are called to deposit seeds of promise in what should be assumed is fertile ground. You don't know what will grow as a result of your effort. The rule is act as if. Act as if this person that may be causing a fuss is a future lawyer, doctor, pastor or president. How one feels internally about their work manifests externally how duties are discharged. Going back to the pessimistic farmer, if he does not believe a bumper crop is on the way, why bother to get up before the sun; why fertilize ground that you think will never yield crops? Here are two stories that illustrate the power of sowing mentoring seeds.

GRANDPA MENTOR

I met my mentee Eddie Silverio when he was 14 years old. He grew up in a neighborhood that was rife with crime and young drug gangs ruled the streets. He joined the youth program I was affiliated with not so much for the opportunity to change but he wanted to meet girls (his account). On one meeting night I went to the men's room and he was in an open stall drinking beer. I looked at him and said the words I try not to use too often, "I am disappointed. I expected more from you." I walked out and returned to my place in the leadership circle. He soon followed me back to the group and sat down. He looked around nervously, not knowing what I was going to do. I never mentioned this incident to my colleagues nor did I bring it up to him.

Fast forward 20 years and my mentee is director of one of the largest and best known Dominican youth programs in northern Manhattan. He invited me to speak to over 700 young people fortunate to have a summer job. His introduction reduced me to tears. He told the group that he wanted to bring up his father (me). He did not say godfather, spiritual father, but father. The young people stood up and clapped. Many spoke to me after the presentation in Spanish, assuming that I could understand them. Going back to the introduction, after the young people stopped clapping; my mentee told the story about our encounter in the restroom. He said that he was never more hurt to know that a person that wanted to help him was now saying he was disappointed in him. We both cried and hugged each other on the stage.

Following this memorable day, I would run into this quirky, diminutive young man, from Eddie's staff named Luis Beltre. He always had a mischievous smile, especially when he called me grandpa mentor (which was every time I would see him). I never really asked why he called me this. I just filed it away in the interesting bin in my mind. A few months after being called grandpa mentor, I asked him why do you refer to me that way? Luis said since I was his mentor's mentor/father figure (Eddie Silverio), it stood to reason that I am his grandpa mentor. It made perfect sense to me. Shortly after this truth was made known, I found out more about my 'grandson' mentee. He ran an education program and was responsible for turning on hundreds of young people from the community to education and college. My 'grandson' mentee was a modern day Pied Piper faithfully leading hard-to-reach youth.

I was not prepared to get a phone call from Eddie telling me that Luis died at the tender age of 24. I asked Eddie for details as my mind wondered how could this happen to a young man. I was told that this extraordinary youth developer had Sickle Cell Anemia. I was further told that Luis would sometimes disappear from the program, usually around his lunch hour, only to be found in the local hospital's emergency room. All of the young people were aware of his suffering and formed an extended family of love and support around him and each other.

A few weeks after Luis died. The street where he lived was named in his memory. He was the youngest person in New York so honored. I had to attend a funeral of a dear friend about 40 miles north of the city that same rainy day of the street dedication. I knew I had to be there to honor the memory of my grandson mentee. I was asked by Eddie to say a few words. I don't recall what was said but when I finished all of our tears joined the 'tears' falling from the sky as the heavens were also mourning. I prayed for Luis' parents. They did not speak one word of English but I felt in my spirit they understood that I was their son's grandpa mentor and I loved him very much.

Months later I was asked by Shawn Dove, then the head of The Mentoring Partnership of New York to help kick off a citywide mentor recruitment effort. I decided to dedicate my presentation to the memory of Luis. I invited his parents (this time they had translators) young people he touched and of course, Eddie. As I stood before the crowd I saw the power of planting a seed in another person. As I prepared to speak, this thought crossed my mind: Don't question the assigned soil; sow your seed where you are and always, like the most optimistic farmer, expect a bumper crop.

I sowed into Eddie. Eddie sowed into Luis. Luis sowed back into both of us and hundreds of young people. He was indeed a blessing and blessed seed sower.

MENTORING TANK

Some years ago I was asked to be a speaker at Sing-Sing Prison (The term The Big House and Going Up The River refers to this institution). As I was seated in the day room, I looked around and saw a young lady who looked familiar. I started talking to her, painfully aware that I knew her but because we were out of a familiar context, I could not quite put my finger on our relationship. I asked, perhaps the dumbest question I could get out my mouth, "What brings you here?" She said she was visiting her husband who was an inmate. I immediately finished the conversation, not wanting to appear insensitive on top of being ignorant.

When I was called up to the podium and was surveying the crowd and was about ready to present, it suddenly dawned on me who this mysterious woman was. We were working together on a community revitalization project in The Highbridge section of The Bronx. She was a community organizer. Her name was Kathy. I felt better punching up her name but my embarrassment over gleaning personal information from her continued rolling around in my mind. While I tried to get this thought out of my head, I started focusing on a rather large inmate who was involved in setting up a musical number before I spoke (like a sermonic selection). I could not take my eyes off of him for some strange reason.

I said to myself, I hope this would not turn into a prison pen pal relationship or if I would have to turn down the usual inmate request to write a letter to the Governor for a pardon or something. I told the Lord, I don't know why you got me focused on this man the inmates and staff called Tank. Before I spoke, Tank sat behind the keyboard and began to sing. I was immediately struck by the tone and power of his soaring voice. He sang, "I Believe I Can Fly"- and I believed, as well as everyone else in the day room, believed he could fly. His song inspired a preachment that I have been blessed to give several times: Locked Up But Never Locked Out. I thought that was the purpose of our non-encounter encounter and I was satisfied to leave it there or so I thought.

At the end of the program I went up to Kathy and found the nerve to ask to meet her husband before I left. To my utter surprise she introduced me to Tank. It was clear that something was going on that I could not question but knew I had to surrender my doubts, suspicion and even fear of getting too deeply involved. I stayed in touch with Tank through his wife while he finished his sentence. He invited me back to Sing-Sing to preach a Palm Sunday word giving new definition to me about the meaning and power of the Resurrection and liberation theology. I found out that Tank was the assistant to the Christian chaplain at Sing-Sing (The prison chaplain was also my Preaching professor at New York Theological Seminary). Tank and I started corresponding and I became godfather to his daughter and an uncle figure to him and his wife.

When Tank was released from prison I was able to get him a job with The Osborne Association where I serve on the Board. In our getting to know each other he told me how he found the Lord in prison. He also talked about getting an education behind bars which included a graduate degree from New York Theological Seminary MPS program (the only program of its kind operating in maximum security prison in America).

Tank was hired to be a leader in an innovative program called Project Uth Turn which sent formerly incarcerated men trained in youth development into churches to mentor at-risk youth. Tank was assigned to Abyssinian Baptist Church in Harlem (a few blocks from where he grew up) under the distinguished leadership of the Rev. Dr. Calvin O. Butts III. It was at this preeminent church that Tank, now I have to say his name and give his proper title, the Rev. Darren Ferguson, became youth pastor and eventually ordained.

It was duing this great time of promise that his beloved Kathy died after a yearlong illness. I thought if there was ever a time for a person to breakdown, give up or do something crazy to get rearrested it was now. Darren and I sometimes talked, cried or sat and said nothing during this painful dark period. It seemed so cruel that this woman who visited him for almost ten years would be called home shortly after his release from prison. Darren got through this crushing period and I am proud to say that a decade after his release from prison Rev. Darren Ferguson serves as Pastor of the Mt. Carmel Baptist Church in Arverne (the Far Rockaway) section of Queens.

He has a youth group that ministers the Word through the creative idiom of combining gospel songs (some written by Rev. Ferguson when he was doing time), spoken word and hip-hop. These young people (also my children) have ministered in many venues around the city and have appeared on television several times. He remarried a lovely and caring woman named Kim. His daughter (my godchild) earned a full scholarship to college, graduated, and is on her way to graduate school. This mentoring relationship, ordained by God, taught me about Divine assignments and how as the old folk would say, "We'll understand it better bye and bye." I am both proud and humbled to be called by God to mentor Tank.

Questions To Ponder

1. Did someone see something positive in you before you could see the same in yourself? If so who was the person and what did they see?

2. Which mentoring story can you relate to as it pertains to either your mentoring style or your life?

3. Can you talk about some mentoring seeds you have sown and describe the 'bumper crop' that has sprung up?

MENTOR'S SPIRITUAL REFLECTION
CREATED TO BEAR FRUIT
Luke 13:6-9

The illustrative story for our lesson is found in The Gospel of Luke. Luke is the most learned disciple. We are told that he is a physician and his comprehensive and insightful writings in Luke and Acts reflect his trained eye and deep mind for detail. Luke's education allowed him to write in flawless Greek which was not easy then or now. The Book of Luke contains many of the parables taught by Jesus to the disciples. Jesus was a master teacher and effectively used parables as a tool to unravel the mysteries of God. A parable is a story that uses common terms known to the hearers in order to explain deep and often hidden truths. Some subjects for parables dealt with: farming, fishing, family, coping with loss, or the uneven relationship between the haves and have-nots. The parables that Jesus taught were offered to bring a supernatural revelatory understanding to a natural mind (without revelation there can be no elevation). This was especially true when Jesus talked about the Kingdom of God.

Come my brothers, let us journey into the text and harvest the richness therein in order to enrich our lives. Let's look closely at the parable. To recount, we are told that a man had a fig tree planted in his vineyard and over the course of three years went to investigate to see if the tree bore fruit. When he did not see any he told the vinedresser to cut down the tree because it was taking up space that a productive tree could benefit. The gardener pleaded for more time and said that he would dig around the tree and fertilize it. The gardener requested that the owner wait one more year and if the tree bares fruit fine and if not then it would be cut down.

Can we unpack the meaning of the parable? The owner of the vineyard is God. The vinedresser or gardener is Jesus. The tree is all of us. God expects us to bear fruit. He expects us to be productive and has given us ample time to develop. It is important to keep in mind that God will not put up with people content to take up space in the vineyard that could be better used by someone else. When the owner of the vineyard says cut down and burn the fruitless trees and plant new trees in their place, Jesus intercedes and pleads for more time. The gardener wants to try more aggressive methods to get the trees to bear fruit. He then says if my intervention works then fine, if not, then cut the tree down and burn the fruitless branches.

Let's zoom in even closer by bringing the parable into current time. There are believers, like fruitless trees, who don't believe what they profess to believe yet they are growing in the vineyard with other trees. *'Believe less'* believers believe that there is no penalty, no sanction, and no personal harm for their faithless actions. They no longer count living a fruitless life as a negative or a big deal perhaps because they forgot or never realized what it feels like to bear fruit. Some men do not believe they deserve to bear fruit. You can't miss what you never had but you can always act like you got it!

Brothers you were not created to live a purposeless life devoid of rhyme, rhythm, reason, shape, tone, texture, value, or meaning. You were not created to exhaust yourself trying to please fruitless people. You were not created to stand alone, be overlooked, be the last, be the least, be a burden, be unappreciated, taking up space, counting time, living in the past or worrying incessantly about the future. You Were Created To Bear Fruit! If God's creation were created to bear fruit, a reasonable question would be, as we look around the community, our home and yes around the church pondering - what happened to the fruit?

In the natural, bad weather can destroy fruit. You hear accounts about how an unexpected cold snap in a place like Florida can damage orange trees. A lack of proper nutrients in the soil can impede the growth of fruit - too much of this and not enough of that can kill a tree. Pestilence like the Asian Boring Beetle can also mess up a tree. Go to Joel and read about how locust stripped a field of everything green. Now that account deals with trees in the natural. What about you? What is going on with your fruit? Unlike the tree, you have free will. That means you have choice where you are rooted because you can move around as you please. With that established, it is important to ask: Are the decisions you make or fail to make killing your fruit? Is the lifestyle you are living bruising your fruit? Do you feel overripe and underappreciated? Are you languishing in the bottom of the fruit basket invisible, ignored and indistinguishable from other fruit? Are the places you choose to go destroying your fruit? Are the people you opt to hang around selectively picking the best of your fruit? Are you self-polluting and thereby participating in the death of your fruit?

There is good news. The vinedresser has experience interceding in fruitless situations and has been granted permission to give you more time to evidence the fruit you were created to bear. The vinedresser is ready, willing and able to take extraordinary measures to help you bear fruit. Since you have free will you have to decide to let him work on you. The longer the fruitless years in your life the more dire the intervention must be. Here are some possible actions the vinedresser may attempt in order to bring forth good fruit out of you:

1. The vinedresser may have to prune back dead branches. The pruning process may seem like cruel and unusual punishment, but the gardener knows that in order for the tree to thrive there must be a loss before there can be a gain.

2. The vinedresser may have to uproot the tree. Have you seen trees that are unnaturally bent due to an encumbrance? Likewise, people can be negatively bent due to constantly pressing up against problems and harmful situations.

3. The vinedresser has to make sure the tree gets plenty of water. I am talking about the living water offered to the Samaritan Woman. This water

satisfies that deep thirst. It can also drown out any unnatural fire burning within.

4. The vinedresser must make sure that the tree gets plenty of light. The light of truth. The light of inner reflection that changes outer direction. The light that has the power to subdue the deepest darkness in and around you.

So brothers what is the evidence that you are bearing good fruit? How do you know what is on the vine is ripe? Come to Galatians 5:22-23 where it talks about the fruit of the Spirit namely: love, joy, peace, patience, kindness, goodness, faithfulness, gentleness and self-control. This is the promised fruit you are expected and were created to bear.

Get past your past and bear fruit. Get over your excuses, illusions, delusions, confusion, fears, doubts, and bear fruit. Get past your inner drought that has dried up hope and possibility and bear fruit. Get over the withering relationship that wounded you to your core and bear fruit. Get through that burning anger and bear fruit. Come up out of the pit of depression so you can bear fruit. Let go of cigarettes, alcohol and drugs that are polluting your body and bear fruit. Get rid of the rotten apples living in your barrel that are spoiling your aspirations, dreams and promise and bear fruit. Get rid of that deeply rooted negative attitude - that nasty way of behaving; thoughts of being better than everyone else; or worse than everyone else and bear fruit. Let go and let God. Let go of whatever you are holding on to that is killing you so you can bear good fruit.

Lift your limbs high to the heavens and begin to praise the Lord in advance for good fruit that is on the way. Let the vinedresser take care of your fruitless situation, your fruitless problem, your fruitless job, your fruitless family situation. Have faith in the vinedresser. He has seen all manner of fruitless conditions. He has seen limbs that were once badly damaged now bearing good fruit. He has seen neglected trees bear fruit. He has witnessed bruised and badly diseased trees bear fruit. He is the master vinedresser and no tree is beyond reclamation. The parable states that the vinedresser said give me one more year. So much can happen in a year. Perhaps this is the year that you will bring forth the fruit you were created to bear!

MENTOR'S MISSION FUEL
DEFEATING POWER BLOCKERS: THE WORD VS. WEEDS
But you shall have power when the Holy Ghost comes upon you. Acts 1:8a

Much of what we hear in church and we tell others is that we have the power to resist the devil. What about when a man feels that he cannot resist and he is being turned out? What happened to the power? My wife has a theory that the power is present but it is being blocked. Power Blockers are like spiritual weeds that are planted (pain) and watered (tears) that choke and ultimately kill your spiritual flowers. Just when you think your inner weeds are gone, they pop up in another place. The only way to defeat Power Blocker Weeds is by sprinkling a heavy dose of *Weed Killing Word* on your inner ground.

Here are some scriptures that can help when your power to resist the following occurs:

Fear

> *The Lord is my light and my salvation; Whom shall I fear? The Lord is the strength of my life; Of whom shall I be afraid?... Though an army may encamp against me, My heart shall not fear; Though war may rise against me, In this I will be confident. Psalm 27:1, 3 NKJV*

Inability to Trust

> *Trust in the Lord with all your heart; and lean not on your own understanding; in all your ways acknowledge him and he will make your paths straight. Proverbs 3:5-6*

Lack of Confidence/Courage

I can do all things through Christ who strengthens me. Philippians 4:13 NKJV

Procrastination

Go to the ant you sluggard; consider its ways and be wise! It has no commander, no overseer or ruler, yet it stores its provisions in summer and gathers its food at harvest. How long will you lie there, you sluggard? When will you get up from your sleep? Proverbs 6:6-9

Lack of Focus

Be joyful always; pray continually; give thanks in all circumstances, for this is God's will for you in Christ Jesus. Do not put out the Spirit's fire; do not treat prophecies with contempt. Test everything. Hold on to good. Avoid every kind of evil. 1 Thessalonians 5: 16-22

Abandonment Issues

I am persuaded that neither death nor life, nor angels nor principalities nor powers, nor things present, nor things to come, nor height nor depth, nor any other created thing, shall be able to separate us from the love of God which is in Christ Jesus our Lord. Romans 8:38-39 NKJV

Worry

So do not worry, saying, 'What shall we eat?' or 'What shall we drink?', or 'What shall we wear?'... But seek first his kingdom and his righteousness and all these things will be given to you as well. Therefore do not worry about tomorrow, for tomorrow will worry about itself. Each day has enough trouble of its own. Matthew 6: 31, 33-34

Feeling Stuck

Forget the former things; do not dwell on the past. See, I am doing a new thing! Now it springs up; do you not perceive it? I am making a way in the desert and streams in the wasteland. Isaiah 43:18-19

Now go, armed with the word and uproot the Power Blockers that threaten the divine/destined bountiful harvest that God desires for us. And men a special request; please don't forget to fire the 'old' gardener!

Questions to Ponder

1. If you had to pick one of the Power Blockers listed which one gets in your way?

2. Is there a Power Blocker not mentioned that gives you trouble (find a weed-whacking scripture)?

3. What would you want to say to the 'old' gardener you fired and how was he able to keep his job for so long?

MENTOR'S TESTIMONY
PLANTING THE SEED - EVERY SEED COUNTS
By Rev. David Joshua Modiega

Reverend David J. Modiega, born in Soweto, is Founder and President of Churches United Against HIV/AIDS (CUAHA). The CUAHA network is a united and coordinated effort by over 40 Southern and Eastern African and Finnish churches and faith-based organizations to scale up and improve the work to address the HIV epidemic and to improve the lives of millions of people living with the virus. CUAHA has partnerships with Anglican, Catholic, Lutheran, Methodist, African Methodist Episcopal, Orthodox and Pentecostal churches, NGO's, non-denominational groups, and multi-faith movements in Angola, Botswana, Ethiopia, Kenya, Malawi, Namibia, Rwanda, South Africa, Swaziland, Tanzania, Uganda, Zambia, Zimbabwe and Finland.

My father's name was Moses and being called Joshua to me was more spiritual and a sign of passing the baton in the biblical sense in the order of my life. My father ended his spiritual journey a Catholic. To get to this meant finding himself. He started out as an Anglican while working in Johannesburg. As he was not fulfilled, he attended the African spiritual church and became a catechist in the Catholic church. One can only hope that his spiritual journey taken as a child can shape and sharpen our focus on what church is all about. It's a seed that is necessary to build a stronger bond with the Lord.

My father was a man of discipline and integrity. He committed to bringing up a God fearing family, so at no point did he spare the rod because it was always about being truthful and honest. When my father passed on in 1978 I was 18 years old. I was about to sit my final year at High School. I wrote the exams but had to assume the role of head of the family and get a job as the first born of 5 siblings (who were all in school at the time). I sacrificed University to emulate what my father did for the family, namely: clothe, feed, pay bills and school fees. My mother was not working and never worked from the time my father died. At this time it was commitment and sacrifice for the family and for a better life.

After my father's death I had another father figure in my godfather Archbishop Walter Khotso Makhulu of the Anglican Church. He relocated to Botswana from Geneva where he was working for the World Council of Churches (WCC) to become a Bishop. In brief, his work with the church and the ecumenical world exposed him to working at the World Council of Churches. He was the President of The All Africa Conference of Churches, As the Archbishop of Central Africa he covered Zimbabwe, Malawi, Botswana and Zambia. His leadership showed me that dealing with people under difficult circumstances and in need was not a job but a passion. If you see God in the next person you will go out of your way to help them no matter what the problem.

The Archbishop escaped from South Africa to work in Botswana in the early 1960's. During this time he helped young people and adults running away from the South African [apartheid] Government to find shelter in countries like Zimbabwe, Zambia and Tanzania as refugees. It is at this time I picked up compassion and humility to deal with various challenges. I learned tough decision-making skills and how to be innovative because of the changing landscape in dangerous situations. To be a successful leader you need to be a servant and humble yourself in love to serve. I seem to have lived in the shadow of great men who suffered to serve the greater good... humanity. In the context of the above I have served churches in Africa and overseas.

I have worked with HIV infected and affected people and with people on the run (refugees). I have seen suffering in Rwanda after the genocide. One cannot always believe that the conscience of humans can be so low as to commit such gruesome killings. Let me say this, when you see people scavenging in a smelly place you may never think that greatness can come out of it. I have helped countless young people realize their dreams from such situations. It is all about love, commitment, compassion and integrity of life. It's not a job. Time and exposure makes that seed grow in you. It depends on you how you actualize it. It is not what you say but what you do that makes people formulate an opinion of you. We are not perfect but one can only do the best with the opportunities prevailing and the seeds they are given.

CHAPTER EIGHT

MENTOR'S SEVEN LIFE LESSONS: PERCEPTION VS. REALITY

Anyone who listens to the word but does not do what it says is like a man that looks at his face in the mirror and, after looking at himself, goes away and immediately forgets what he looks like. James 1:23-24

It has become increasingly difficult for youth and adults alike to distinguish between what is real and what is a fake. This problem is reinforced by high definition software that can create reality. Photoshop pictures can place a person in any setting surrounded by an unknown cast of characters. Technology allows a person to go online and create an imaginary persona that can have dire consequences to the unsuspecting. If you desire to discern the role perception plays in influencing reality I want you to know that you are already moving in the right direction.

Some folk will be forever stuck battling what appears to be real. For example if a person believes he will never find a satisfying job because of a perceived lack on his part the perception can become real. If he never bothers to look for a job this is called a self-fulfilling prophesy when a person believes something negative will happen and then creates the climate for this dreaded act to occur. Perception can actually be as powerful as reality if a person truly believes what he perceives to be true. This is why it is important to understand the role perception plays in life. With this said I want to present Seven Life Lessons (LL) on how to successfully distinguish perception from reality.

LL # 1

All that glitters is not gold. In the middle-ages there were people called alchemists. They thought *they* could take base metals like tin and lead and turn them into gold. Some people today are like the alchemists. They look at a glittery object and automatically assume this must be gold. If you spend most of your time making excuses for a person in a vain attempt to make him or her look better in your eyes and others you are trying to turn a base metal into gold. Likewise, if your "heart" is made out of tin but you have tricked yourself into believing it is gold, you have managed to fool yourself. Self-deception is never a good thing.

LL # 2

Learn to differentiate between wants and needs. It is possible to want something but not need it. My mom once told me, "People will buy what they want and beg for what they need." A person may want a car but what he really needs to do is first find a job. Another example is a man may want a loving relationship but won't stop playing the field. Wants and needs confusion is rampant and can contribute to more misperception which triggers a new cycle of wants and needs.

LL # 3

It is not where you start out in life it is where you end up. If your perception tells you over and over again that it is too late, that you wasted too much time, that other people are smarter than you that is why they were able to overcome and move on - KNOW THAT YOU HAVE MIND-CHECKED YOURSELF. I know people bloom at different times. One common misconception is that there is a definable right time. There is a better time for sure, but I don't know about a quintessential right time.

LL # 4

Everybody that is moving is not necessarily going somewhere. It is possible to move and not travel. There are some folk you may know that get up, leave the house, move around, but at the end of the day they are in the same spot. These folk look like everyone else, they wear the latest clothes, they say 'son' all the time - they even talk about the future. If you stop looking and start seeing you will soon discover that you don't see anything at all.

LL # 5

One of the hardest life lessons to learn is that you can learn lessons from life. If you lead an unexamined life you are not learning vital lessons about life from life. If your perception is that you and everybody in your family got bad luck then you will attribute consequences for your decisions to powers that you can't see but yet this power has negative control over you. It is hard to look at what you can't see. It is more difficult to defeat what you can't see. You see?

LL # 6

Find a pair of invisible scissors. Please don't think that my perception is off because I mentioned invisible scissors. If you don't believe in these scissors then you will also believe that you can't cut away from negative people, destructive places or cut loose things that are not serving you well. If you are with dead beats that don't want to go anywhere or do anything take out your scissors and go SNIP SNIP. If you are hanging with dream killers it is time to SNIP SNIP. If you are tired of folk who are leeches forever taking and never giving, go SNIP SNIP...

LL # 7

Please write your own perception life lesson that you have learned. It could be recent or in your past.

Questions to Ponder

1. Do you remember when you thought something or someone was real only to discover that this was not the case? How did the change in perception happen?

2. Why do you think it is/was difficult for you not to perceive danger even when other people warned you?

3. If you could go back in time and use your magic scissors what period would you journey to and what would you like to SNIP SNIP?

MENTOR'S SPIRITUAL REFLECTION
BOOT CAMP FOR SPIRIT WARRIORS
Ephesians 6:10-18

How many of you know that there is a war going on? I'm not talking about natural wars around the world. I'm referring to the war in the heavens. This war is between the forces of light vs. the minions of darkness. A war pitting good against evil, love vs. hate. This on-going war, waged by the "ungod" since time immemorial, has killed the hopes, dashed the dreams, blunted possibilities and obliterated the spirit of countless men. Well brothers, my orders from headquarters could not be clearer: Seek out and recruit men willing to fight the enemy in the streets, in the home, community, on the job, and in the church. There is a crying need for Spirit Warriors who will not give up the fight.

You should know that while many are called only a few will be chosen. We are looking for men who are willing to be relieved of pew sitting duty and will march to the frontlines. There is a deep need for men willing to deny their flesh and enroll in Special Forces Boot Camp to become a Spirit Warrior. Hear me now you can't become a Spirit Warrior by osmosis. You have to be willing to give in order to get. You must have keen eyes that see out as well as see inwardly. You can't become a Spirit Warrior by merely sitting next to, or hanging out with a Spirit Warrior. You will not be admitted to this elite boot camp because you got pull. You may very well be the first in your tribe to enlist, or your daddy or great granddaddy may have been Spirit Warrior generals. No matter. You will have to earn your stripes by suffering stripes each and every day.

I want to introduce you to the Spirit Warrior Drill Instructor. Please know that this leader is battle tested. He knows the way of the enemy because he was once a star soldier with an extraordinarily dark future with the other side. He was born Saul of Tarsus, but you can call him by his Spirit Warrior name, Apostle Paul, denoting both rank and respect. Some of you may still have doubts concerning if Apostle Paul is a bona fide choice. You may have trouble forgetting that he once held the cloaks of those religious men who stoned to death a great Spirit Warrior named Stephen. Some may say that Paul is not fit for leadership because he did several bids in prison or that he constantly complains about a thorn in his flesh. If you still are not convinced that Paul is worthy then perhaps this is not for you. But for those gung-ho brothers, I ask, are you ready to go?

If you are going to be a Spirit Warrior the first rule of engagement is that you must master discovering who your real enemy is. You will never defeat what you fail to recognize! That is why when you do soul patrol duty you shout: "Halt Who Goes There?" You must know your enemy because your enemy surely knows you. Your enemy is not your wife. Your enemy is not your children, your next of kin, or your boss. Your enemy is not the father who may have left you or the man who abused you. Your enemy is not the brother sitting next to you because your enemy is not flesh and blood! Your enemy is an ungodly spirit, seeking whom it can destroy. Your adversary will always use doubt, confusion, anger, jealousy and fear to help you fight fake enemies that exist in your mind. You are not a danger to Satan's kingdom when you blindly fight faux (fake) foes. You are more apt to hurt innocent bystanders (friendly fire) rather than your true unholy accuser.

I encourage you to make room for the spiritual knowledge you will need to operate behind enemy lines. You must purge your pain, brokenness, hurts, mistakes; toss all of it in the sea of forgetfulness. The more gunk, funk and junk you jettison from your life's trunk, the more spiritual knowledge you can obtain and take with you on the battlefield of life. You can't fight this war with just testosterone. You can't "man up" or out trash talk this devil. It is impossible to outspend, out hustle, out curse, or out fake your adversary. It is not possible to out bling, out psyche, out drink, out smoke, out inject, out hang, out bang, out freak, out lie or outlive the devil.

The Apostle Paul's boot camp has only two grades - Pass or Fail. There are some men who have failed out of boot camp but they have learned enough of the lingo to fool folk in and out of the church. Just because there are men in church does not mean that church is in them. So beware of double-agents. Here are some mandatory classes you must pass in order to become a Spirit Warrior:

Gym Class—Paul used sports as a way to relate and teach men. He said to the men of Ephesus, "We wrestle not against flesh and blood but spiritual wickedness in high places." He told Timothy, Fight the good fight of faith." He told the people of Philippi, "Press toward the mark of the prize of the high calling."

Psyche Class—Paul was the master of understanding the mind (before Freud, Jung, Billingsley or Pouissant). He knew that the enemy's imps are tactically trained to leave some good in your heart while taking good out of your mind. Look at what Dr. Paul says in Romans 12:2: "Be not conformed to this world but be transformed by the renewing of your mind." Hear and understand this subtle truth: In order to change you must transform but just because you change does not automatically mean you have been transformed.

Social Studies—Paul teaches about the greatest weapon in a Spirit Warriors arsenal found in 1Corinthians 13:4-8. It is not hate. It is not brute force. It is love that is: patient, kind, not envious or boastful, arrogant or rude. A love that does insist on its own way; it is not irritable or resentful; it does not rejoice in wrong doing. A love rejoices in truth. A love that bears all things, believe all things, hopes for all things; a true love that never fails. A Spirit Warrior must master being a love commando!

Study Hall—A Spirit Warrior must spend time alone. When separated from others either by choice or circumstance think on these things: Whatsoever things are true, honorable, just, pure, pleasing, or commendable. And while you are thinking mull this over: When I was a child I thought as a child but when I became a man I put away childish things. If you want to be a mature Spirit Warrior you must be willing to put away childish things, childish excuses, and childish evaluations/observations.

If you got this far, you are now ready to receive your Spirit Warrior uniform. I am talking about the Helmet of Salvation, The Breastplate of Righteousness, The Sword of the Spirit and The Shield of Faith. But wait a minute. Don't make the mistake of thinking that the power is in the gear. There are apprentice Spirit Warriors who LOVE to dress up for the outward battle before properly attending to the inward battle. Apostle Paul said it this way: "The good I would do I do not and the evil that I don't want to do that is what I do." Spirit Warriors can I drop this counter-intuitive thought on you? Before you can successfully and consistently attack the external enemy you have to first persistently combat and attack the internal enemy. Your chief protagonist can be you. There are some things that we cannot always blame on the devil. It can be you and the devil. If you defeat one and not the other you may erroneously think you are ready to graduate from boot camp.

This is War! Please don't try to appease your enemy, minimize your foe, make side deals, fight today's battles with yesterday's tactics, or flat out compromise with the Prince of Lies. Whatever peace you may seem to have bought in the short term know that all hell is about to break loose in the long term. Now hear this, you shouldn't go through blood, sweat and tears to become a Spirit Warrior and be content to sit in the congregation, arms folded, wondering when the sermon will end, what the crab grass is doing or if a pigeon soiled your automobile parked outside.

My brothers in struggle, I am so glad we have a Supreme Commander. He is more than a Bishop, Archbishop, Pope or Apostle. He is battled-tested like no other. The forces of darkness took him down in a hole and was about to claim immoral victory over Him, but they could not take him out. He got up with all power in His hands. For the men who have willingly taken and passed the Apostle Paul's Boot Camp classes; and have mastered the art of internal and external warfare; and have repented of your sins; and have made room for the indwelling of the Holy Ghost, you are ready for our Supreme Commander to issue your Spirit Warrior field commission. Hear his words from Acts 1:8:

> *"But you will receive power when the Holy Ghost comes on you; and you will be my witnesses in Jerusalem and in all Judea and Samaria, and to the ends of the earth."*

MENTOR'S MISSION FUEL
SEVEN PRINCIPLES:
MOVING FROM ORDINARY TO EXTRAORDINARY

1. You must have a consistent, identifiable, guiding, liberating, and empowering life vision/philosophy inspired by The Holy Spirit that encompasses your private, personal and professional life governing how you interact with family colleagues, friends, and self.

2. Associate with people who desire to elevate and not denigrate you or other people that may not measure up to a set of ostracizing capricious standards. Avoid at all cost: Dream Killers, Ph.D.'s of Negativity, Water Cooler Malcontents, Drama/Trauma Kings and Queens and the Perpetually Depressing Folk.

3. Practice treating people the way you would like to be treated *(not necessarily the way you have been treated!)*. The underlying assumption is that you want the best for yourself and that you have learned how to be your best friend.

4. Some men have grown adept at <u>preying</u> as a residue of the hunter/gatherer gene. What is not as easy for men to do is pray silently or corporately (out loud in front of a group): for self, family, situations and others. And please don't think the only place to pray is in church. Men, you must pray at home with and for your loved ones.

5. Don't forget where you came from or where you are destined to go. Don't be reticent to tell your story. Always lift others as you climb; remember to whom much is given, much is required. Generously share your love, wisdom, joy and vision. Create room for people to know and grow; and always be willing to hear a story before telling a story.

6. Be proactive and not reactive. Yesterday is done. You can't change the past. You can use life lessons from the past to impact your present which changes your future. Vow to live and learn from the good, the bad and ugly

in others and in self. Don't forget to ask, "Is it really me?"

7. Do not neglect your mind, body (rest) or Spirit. Do what refreshes you like: a hobby, exercise, cooking, reading or doing nothing (hard for some people). And by all means don't forget to meditate on the scriptures and pray.

Questions to Ponder

1. Looking over the list of Moving From The Ordinary to The Extraordinary which number is your greatest challenge to date. Why?

2. Have you ever met a Dream Killer while growing up? Who was this person and how did he or she assassinate your dream?

3. If you could ask yourself a question that has not been asked in this entire book what would you ask yourself? And what would the answer be? Remember to go deep.

MENTOR'S TESTIMONY
UNCLE JEAN DENIS – MY FIRST MENTOR
By Steve Vassor MSSA

Steve Vassor is a husband, father, mentee and mentor with 20 years of service to young people and the communities where they live. He was raised in D.C. He now worships at Epworth United Methodist Chapel in Baltimore, Maryland. Steve works with the United Way of Southeastern Pennsylvania's Center for Youth Development, where the team he leads strives to ensure that all young people, with an emphasis on Black males, graduate high school prepared for college, career and life.

Uncle Jean (pronounced "zhahn") immigrated to the US from Haiti in the early 1970's. When he first arrived, he and my grandfather lived in a rented studio apartment in NW Washington DC. He graduated with honors from Cardozo HS, and went on to study electrical engineering at the University of the District of Columbia (UDC). After leaving UDC, he joined NASA's Goddard Space Flight Center as one of the only Black electrical engineers focused on jet propulsion engines at that time.

While in college, and as soon as he was old enough to move out on his own, Jean rented a one-bedroom bachelor's pad and furnished it with a stereo system, a second-hand sofa and a bookshelf made of cinder blocks and wood planks. That bookshelf held advanced calculus books, college level geometry texts, FORTRAN, COBOL and BASIC manuals, dictionaries in four languages, history books, two Bibles and pictures of the family. It also held yellowed copies of Alex Haley's *Roots* and *The Autobiography of Malcolm X.* It was from this makeshift bookshelf that I was first introduced to Malcolm X's story.

In 1979, Uncle Jean gave me my first hip-hop record as a birthday gift. It was a fresh (brand-new, sealed, and very nice) copy of Rapper's Delight, the seminal classic by the Sugar Hill Gang. I had recently seen them perform on Soul Train, heard the record playing on radios throughout the neighborhood, and now had my own personal copy. As I look back now, the true gift of that record was twofold – first, it started my lifelong love of hip-hop music; second, he used it and other music to teach me about his personal soundtrack that included the music he grew up with as a boy in Haiti, and the music he grew to love as a young man in the USA. He and I analyzed and studied the life, lyrics and music of Robert Nestor ("Bob") Marley, and how these all applied to the Black Diaspora. Before these and other conversations I didn't realize how important and interconnected Black people were. Through musicians such as Bob Marley, Fela, and Coltrane, Uncle Jean taught me that African and Black history were more than Africa, slavery, Black History month, emancipation and the Civil Rights movement.

A few years later, after a few bad decisions that led to a particularly bad episode, my very worried, tired, angry parents sent me to Jean's place. I wasn't too worried about disappointing my parents, but mortified about what my uncle might say. On that evening, there was no Marley, no radio, no discussion of the Black Diaspora. His words to me were "you know you're **&@&%!*+* up right? Why are you TRYING to &$%#@*&^ up?" After which, he stopped speaking and went back to studying calculus. Those words stung then and even today because they were the harshest ones he had used towards me. AND he was right.

Though I didn't know what a mentor was, Jean was mine. He encouraged without being a cheerleader; he challenged me without cajoling or lectures. He shared his knowledge in ways that were not demeaning of me, and used music, books and current events as a way to enter and engage me in discussions. His mentorship is still an influence, and has guided the way I work with young people.

CHAPTER NINE

MENTOR'S FACEBOOK PAGE—AN OPEN BOOK?

For nothing is secret that will not be revealed, nor anything hidden that will not be known and come to light. Luke 8:17 (NKJV)

The growth of social media has impacted societal life and relationships in a remarkable, lasting and sometimes disturbing way. Most young people that you may mentor have been raised in a time when technology was always present. It is as ubiquitous as television was for an earlier generation. No matter what your feelings about social media; if you are on Facebook or not, it is important for you to grasp the power that is influencing behavior of young and not-so-young alike. You may have already opted to use a social media platform or converse with your mentee via email (if allowed by the mentoring program and family).

So here are some thoughts on social networking that could be helpful especially if you are from the generation that marveled when Neil Armstrong took "One small step for man, a giant step for mankind (remember that?)." I read an article in The New York Times Magazine (July 25, 2010) titled *The End of Forgetting* by Jeffery Rosen. The author astutely presented how personal comments/pictures sent to web based sites like Facebook, MySpace, Google, YouTube, blogs or Twitter can in theory live forever in cyberspace. This reality has ominous implications for boastful, too truthful, unmindful, malicious or scandalous posts as human resource professionals, banks, college admission counselors and Pastors are all going online for posted information.

There was a time when this sort of intense scrutiny was reserved for celebrities, but now, thanks to technology, the cycle of fame has extended way beyond 15 minutes as predicted by Andy Warhol. Now your deeds, good, bad or indifferent can live forever. Old fashioned office gossip once took place around the water cooler among nosey co-workers. The most itching ear back then could not spread salacious news but so far or fast. The water cooler has been replaced by the computer screen and scurrilous stories can just as easily make their way around an office community, church, or around the world. This Orwellian reality (Read *1984* by George Orwell) also has consequences for members of the faith community.

There was a time when brothers and sisters confessed to the Lord their innermost issues and dark secrets (sins). Now confessions (as well as accusations) are posted online for all to see. It begs the question who is the real you – the pew you or the online you? What is it about technological notoriety that will allow a person to share their foibles, miscues, spicy private photos - or at the other end of the spectrum, their boring and mundane life routines with the universe? Is it really that important to let people know you are sleepy? Or that your shower water was not as hot as yesterday? To be fair there is a positive role social networks play in bringing friends and families together especially when distance is a factor; sharing information and ideas or organizing an event like a high school reunion.

I reluctantly joined Facebook after hearing that some of my mentees, without my knowledge, started Reverend Alfonso Wyatt Is My Mentor page. I read the comments (I am up to 100 friends) of people I was blessed to help, encourage or minister to over the last decade to the present. I could clearly see and feel the cyber attraction that keeps track of the number of friends that visit you (what ever happened to pen pals?) and the desire to 'hit' someone back long into the night or most of the day. It was disconcerting when mentees began to ask to be friends and if you don't respond, they now think you are no longer friends. All in all, I exited the site happy that there was nothing posted that I would be embarrassed for my mother to see.

As mentioned, some of you may mentor young people who came of age thinking that the Internet was here forever. Children born during this rapidly changing technological era view change as normal while their elders either struggle to keep up or never got into the 'moving at the speed of the Internet' pace. It will be difficult to truly understand the full dimension of young people and youth culture without understanding, if not embracing, social media. I am not prescribing that mentors get on Facebook or Tweet as the sole way of conversing with their mentee.

Times change and flexible people find ways to keep up by changing with the times.

It is important to say that social media, computer games and hours surfing the Internet can never be allowed to become a substitute for meaningful family, human interaction or emotional exchange. Call me old school but I am amazed that couples will go out to dinner and spend most of their time between bites (bytes) communicating with someone else. Perhaps that person on the other end of the call, text or Tweet should have been invited to dinner. Brother David Miller, a friend and colleague from Baltimore, has become a national spokesman for a movement called Power Down. It is a reminder to parents to monitor and regulate the use of technology in the home. One of Miller's more brilliant ideas is calling for a family technology fast on specific weekends. The thought behind Power Down is that it will allow time for meaningful family interaction.

Mentors, if you are on Facebook the question must be asked what would your mentee see if he looked for you online? Remember the early Chapter that talked about character? It said that character is the real you when no one is looking. An unguarded posting on Facebook could undue years of mentor/mentee hard work. Facebook is truly an open book. Not to believe or understand this fact could be injurious to your reputation and relationship with your young charge. If you are online in any way you can be an open target for anyone who has a beef with you or have other issues that have nothing to do with you. I recall going on the Facebook page of a friend and co-laborer in the Gospel. I saw that he received a suggestive post from an over amorous and well-endowed pursuer. It was shocking to say the least. I made a low tech move and called a mutual friend that had his number to warn him what was happening on his wall (which he seldom checked). He was horrified, embarrassed and angered to see and read what was there for the world to see, read - and judge.

There is now software called Reputation Defender designed to police the Internet for a price to make sure that any disparaging remarks are not transmitted without a customer's knowledge. Reputation Defender knows how to bury unflattering statements in the depths of Google's basement or remove it altogether. There was a time that God was the ultimate reputation defender. He would take sinners and forgive and forget all that was said or done in the past. In fact, we are told that our sins are tossed in the sea of forgetfulness there to rise no more. Facebook, MySpace (even I know this has fallen off the tech radar screen), your favorite blog or an indiscriminate text, email or Tweet cannot forgive nor forget. So the techno/existential question boils down to this: Which book do you really want to be in forever - Facebook or The Lamb's Book? Tweet that question please and I pray it goes viral.

Questions to Ponder

1. If your mentee looked you up on Facebook is what you say electronically about yourself consistent with what you say every day about yourself?

2. Have you ever used any form of social media to stay in touch with your mentee? If so how did it work?

3. If you could capture one of your proudest moments in life and allow it to play on YouTube, what would you like the world to see?

MENTOR'S SPIRITUAL REFLECTION
YEARNING FOR A SECOND CHANCE
Luke 22:31-34, 54-62

All of us at one time in our lives would have to fess up that we have messed up. We all could be found guilty of having done something that we are not proud of; said something that we wish we could take back; or witnessed something that we could have stopped. We have had opportunities that we did not take full advantage of; stayed in negative situations far longer than we should; or wasted time. We have told lies when we should have told the truth. We took something or someone that did not belong to us.

Somebody can't get a person, an event, a misdeed, an action, a lapse in judgment out of their mind.

There is a brother carrying a burden, a weight that has slowed you down, or has stopped you from progressing thereby stunting your mental, social and spiritual growth. Something is eating at you; causing you to lose sleep. This thing is negatively impacting your relationship with family and friends. If you see yourself in one of these categories or you have managed to still hide your mess-ups, please know that this word is for you. It would not be true to life if we never yearned for a second chance; a 'do over', an opportunity to set something straight that went horribly wrong.

This is a good time to go to the text. We zoom in on a time in Peter's life that he wished he could take back; a time when his words did not match his actions. We are told that Jesus warned Peter that the devil was on his tracks and that despite his past bravado, the enemy desired to sift him like wheat. Jesus went on to say to Peter that before the rooster crows you will deny me three times - not once, not twice, but three times. Don't you wonder what was going through Peter's mind when he heard that he would betray Jesus? Peter being Peter probably thought that he was ready to go all the way even to prison and death as he asserted earlier. Let's focus on Peter. What we know about him is the following:

- His name was Simon and he hailed from Galilee the same area where Jesus was born (Galilee was synonymous in the eyes of Jews from Judea with being unlearned, a fool, a heathen, sinner or worse).

- He made his living as a fisherman. Jesus told Simon and his brother Andrew, "Follow me and I will make you fishers of men."

- His name was changed by Jesus from Simon to Peter which means rock. Jesus went on to say, "Upon this rock I will build my church."

- Peter tentatively walked on water and was the first to acknowledge that Jesus was indeed the Christ.

Peter had another side to him like many men in and out of the church. Peter had an explosive temper. It was Peter that pulled out a small sword and took off a man's ear in the Garden of Gethsemane when a mob came to arrest Jesus. It was Peter that forbade the Lord from washing his feet but later relented after being rebuked by Jesus.

The stage is set for what has to be the lowest point of Peter's life. Jesus has been placed under arrest and is now being severely beaten. Peter stays nearby but not too close; he is in the vicinity of Jesus. While he is in the courtyard a young girl spies Peter and starts to yell, "I know this man he was with him." Peter said, "Woman, I don't know him." Another person said the same thing and Peter again denied knowing Jesus. Yet a third man an hour later says "certainly this fellow was with Him for he is Galilean."

Peter, perhaps feeling the heat, swears an oath (curse) that he does not know Jesus. All three Gospels give evidence of this occurrence but only Luke makes this keen observation. He says that as the Lord passed by He looked straight at Peter. Peter then remembered what Jesus said to him earlier, "Before the roster crows you will deny me three times." Jesus looked at Peter when Peter refused to look at him, to own him, to stand beside him.

What kind of look did Peter see: was it a sad look of disappointment? Or was it one of those you of all people looks? Was it a cutting look of betrayal? Was it you and Judas are cut from the same cloth kind of look? Was it a contrite look of defeat suggesting, hey Peter they got me so you may as well keep up with the charade? There is no sense of both of us getting busted. Was it a convincing look that was to reassure Peter that this is all in the plan? We will never know exactly what type of look it was but we know the impact it had on Peter. All four Gospels state that after seeing Jesus and hearing the cock crow, Peter wept bitterly. The story could have ended with Peter broken, angry and depressed over what transpired.

But the Good News is that we serve a God of second chances. Let's look at Jesus' words expressed earlier to Peter:

"Simon, Simon, Satan has asked to sift you like wheat. But I have prayed for you, Simon that your faith may not fail. And when you have turned back, strengthen your brothers." Luke 22:31

Imagine Jesus praying for you before a mess up, during a mess up or after a mess up. When Jesus prays something has to happen; something has to change. I believe that was what the look back to Peter was all about. Not to condemn him but to encourage him to not give up; to not go down into the pit of self-pity.

It was the same Peter after Pentecost that preached his trial sermon and 3000 souls gave their lives to Christ. It was the forgiven Peter that became a revered Apostle and convinced fellow Jews to allow Gentiles (me and you) into the Christian fold. Peter yearned for a second chance as he wept. We discover that his setback was the stage for a divinely inspired comeback.

Read Peter's second chance words:

"To this you were called because Christ suffered for you, leaving you an example that you should follow in his steps. He committed no sin, and no deceit was

found in his mouth. When they hurled their insults at him, he did not retaliate; when he suffered, he made no threats. Instead, he entrusted himself to him who judges justly. He himself bore our sins in his body on the tree, so that we may die to sins and live for righteousness; by his wounds you have been healed. For you were like sheep going astray, but now you have returned to the Shepherd and Overseer of your souls."
1Peter 2:21-25

Peter made the most of his second chance. How about you?

Mentor's Testimony
REACHING UP FOR MANHOOD
Reprinted By Permission
By Geoff Canada

Geoffrey Canada, born in The South Bronx, is an educational reformer, leading the Harlem Children's Zone, a hugely ambitious network of charter schools renowned for its cradle-to-college approach. Mr. Canada, who created The Harlem Children's Zone in 1997, manages the first and so far the only organization in the country that pulls together under a single umbrella integrated social and educational services for thousands of children at once. President Obama created a grant program to copy Mr. Canada's block-by-block approach to ending poverty. The British government praised his charter school as a model and invited him to speak to Parliament. The documentary "Waiting for 'Superman' " revolves around Mr. Canada. Mr. Canada, who holds a master's degree from the Harvard Graduate School of Education, has achieved superhero status among those who admire him for the breadth of his vision. He has appeared on 60 Minutes more than presidents and world leaders. Geoff Canada, a life-time martial artist has used this art form to mentor and transform the lives of hundreds of young people since the early 80's. Many are still in his life today.

If we are going to save the next generation of young boys, they need to be connected to men so they see examples of the possible futures they may live out as adults. At the same time, we have to be careful that we do not go charging into children's lives without being properly prepared for the different way they see the world. It's as much an issue of class and culture as it is race.

This is not a call for people not to get involved in mentoring but just the opposite. I think all of us must do more to help children at risk, especially our boys. Mentoring is a critical activity that can help support children and can make the difference between a child succeeding or failing. It is my belief that the most powerful force in a child's life is a caring adult and that we must get involved personally if we are going to change the outcomes for those children who face the most difficulties. But unless we are already trained to work with children, we must start slowly. We must understand that children growing up in impoverished circumstances often have a worldview difficult for some adults to comprehend but totally consistent with their life experience. We must spend time understanding what the children with whom we want to work are going through and living with every day.

If this is not understood and factored into our work with children, we can easily create situations that do more harm than good. The gap between the poor and the non-poor, regardless of race, is growing ever larger in this country. Things many of us take for granted - safety, enough food, decent housing, a trip to the movies - poor children may have to struggle to obtain. This often creates circumstances where conflicts and hurt feelings between children and well-intentioned outsiders occur unintentionally.

I have known so many people who want to do good but are not prepared to work with those they want to help. As any of us who have raised children know, it takes more than love and good intentions to do a good job. There are certain very concrete skills that are necessary in order to work with children. We need to know something about child development, about cultural differences, about the difficulties families face raising children in poverty. This information can be collected from many sources, including local community-based organizations, faith institutions, community leaders, and the children and families themselves.

The sad fact is that in America we have so many poor children of all races who are experiencing similar horrid circumstances in their young lives. We have millions of poor children growing up in homes with single parents who are unable to properly support them, in communities where violence is the norm and not the exception, in schools that have long ago given up on educating them.

When people think about volunteering to help children, they often think about the most at-risk children.

They fail to realize that there is a much larger population of children who are falling through the cracks more gradually, sometimes less dramatically, and that with a helping hand - some attention, some support, some love - from a caring adult, these children could achieve dramatically better outcomes. There are enough children who need our help that each one of us can find the right match, very likely close to home and go to work to build trust and offer support in order to make a real difference in the life of a child.

Excerpt is from *Reaching Up for Manhood: Transforming the Lives of Boys in America* Beacon Press

CHAPTER TEN

MENTOR'S MASTER TEACHING ON FRIENDSHIP

My command is this: Love each other as I have loved you. Greater love has no one than this that he lay down his life for his friends. You are my friends if you do what I command. I no longer call you servants, because a servant does not know his master's business. Instead, I have called you friends, for everything I have learned from my Father I have made known to you. John 15:12-15

Young people spend an inordinate amount of time with their friends. This may not be a bad thing if the friends are positive. Friendships can become problematic when negative peer pressure comes into play. It has been proven that respect and confirmation from peers can counter the best efforts of parents, pastors and mentors. So men it is important to think about your concept of friendship so we can help young people recognize what a healthy friendship looks and feels like. Most of us probably spend more time talking to our friends than talking about friendship. So let's have an open and frank discourse on the subject.

Before starting, we should have a working definition from the dictionary which states a relationship or alliance with another person that *is hopefully mutually beneficial.* Focus on the words hopefully mutually beneficial. It is possible to be in a friendship that is not mutually beneficial. Some would say that this is not true because friends should always be there for each other. If this was always the case then friendships would theoretically never end, at least not on some of the sour notes some people have experienced. To be clear some friendships are destined to last for a defined season. This means there is a specific need/purpose that once met each party moves on with no hurt feelings. It is a special person that is "called" to be a seasonal friend helping troubled people weather life's storms. This type of friend may not always get his or her deserved accolades because of the nature of the issue addressed (usually deeply personal) and the relative short duration of time on task.

Now it could be me but I don't see how every person one befriends can be elevated to the status of best friend. A best friend has the "right" to speak honestly to their friend and never resort to speaking behind their back. These special friendships are not solely bonded on what one can do for the other but is held together by respect, truth and love. A best friend will tell you the truth the whole truth and nothing but the truth and in some instances be willing to risk the friendship in the process. The title of best friend should always be earned and never cavalierly bestowed. The best friend contract takes work on both sides in order for it to be mutually beneficial. If you claim to be a best friend and you are doing all of the giving or all of the taking please keep reading.

There are people that may be called best friends but they are really sycophants. A sycophant is a person that is practiced in the art of currying favor through excessive flattery. By definition this person will never tell the truth because they do not wish to risk whatever secondary gains he or she may receive through their hustle that looks like a relationship. A sycophant cannot be a best friend. They can be a fan at best, and in the worse circumstance, a stalker. Either way the object of their obsequious behavior may be headed for trouble. It is not healthy to have people that are drawn to you by slavish admiration. In fact it is downright creepy.

In all relationships, good, bad or indifferent, needs are being met. The question is what needs are being met between you and your mentees? Do you require and/or encourage mentee sycophants to hang around you? Are you angry when you receive constructive criticism from a mentee or a friend or does it depend on the "status" of the person offering advice? Have you confused having mentees with having friends? These are crucial questions that must be asked if you want an open, honest and healthy relationship. While mentoring is not always rooted in friendship the dynamics can be similar. What type of relationship do you want with your mentee? Is it important that your young charge see you as larger than life? Would you rather have a balanced relationship or do you really want a bunch of sycophants hanging on your every word? I believe how we see friendship plays a role in how we approach mentoring. Again, I am not saying that all mentee relationships end in friendship but when it does it can be quite satisfying to mentor and mentee alike.

Questions to Ponder

1. Who is the first best friend you can remember?

2. Can you recall a friend who exerted a negative influence over you?

3. If you could contact a friend from the past who you have not seen or talked to, who would you want to see and what would be the tenor of your conversation?

MENTOR'S SPIRITUAL REFLECTION
EXPOSING THE GREAT PSYCHER
Luke 4:1-13

Do you remember some of the childhood games you and your friends played like tag, hide-go-seek, hot peas and butter? All of these games depended on physical skill. In short, you had to be able to run in order to excel. But there was another game young people played in the hood that did not require speed of foot, but called for speed of mind. This game was called 'Psyche Yo Mind' The object was to completely fool somebody by getting them to believe the unbelievable. You would say something like this to a friend (usually one who was weak minded) in a hyped voiced, "I saw your 'moms' in the principal's office and he was tellin' her bad stuff about you. I left when I saw her take a big belt out of her pocketbook and she is headed this way!" Just as your poor friend was about to have a nervous breakdown, you yelled, "Psyche Yo Mind!!!"

The devil has been playing "Psyche Yo Mind" head games for a long time except for one important difference- he is not playing. He is trying to get people young and not-so-young to turn their back on God by feeling their situation is hopeless. The enemy takes special delight in fooling young believers. The adversary wants to psyche young people before this Word gets rooted in their belly, or sneakily plant a mess-up seed for a planned delayed bitter harvest. How many of you know that the devil is a master at playing mind games (1st account in Garden of Eden). He can appear like a trusted friend but the adversary is anything but a trusted friend. This diabolical chameleon is psyching people in and out of the church, by first fooling and then getting them to willingly or reluctantly pay the high cost of low living.

Some young people feel as long as they've got a beat or have memorized their favorite rapper's rhymes that they will be alright. In fact, the enemy and his minions have a favorite tune sung by The **Devilphonics on WBFH (Who Bound For Hell)** big hit station. Their number one song is, 'Didn't I Psyche Your Mind This Time"... They dedicate this long playing jam to young and old who find themselves in a jam.

Here are some dedications:

Didn't I Psyche Your Mind This Time when I convinced you that the people who really love you hate you and the people who hate you love you?

Didn't I Psyche Your Mind This Time when I lured you out of the safety of the church and convinced you that you can find safety with a gang or other dysfunctional, low self-esteem, knuckleheads who are miserable and want you to be even more miserable.

Didn't I Psyche Your Mind This Time when I walked into your head and snatched your dreams, turning them into your worst nightmare? I finally convinced you that you can be somebody by being a big nobody.

Didn't I Psyche Your Mind This Time when I convinced you to drop out of school? I encouraged you to laugh at then separate yourself from your old nerdy friends who did not want to steal, rob or destroy – or get high. Those same lames will be future doctors, lawyers, teachers, and. devil forbid - pastors. I know that to be true, too bad you don't.

Didn't I Psyche Your Mind This Time when I got you to believe you can somehow reap life's benefits even if you never sowed seeds in life's garden?

Didn't I Psyche Your Mind when I convinced you that you can stand 24/7 on the corner of Nowhere Street and Hopeless Boulevard, all dressed up with your pants sagging; cussin', fightin', drinkin' and smoking.' I made you believe that you were not jeopardizing your future or damaging your mind... All I can say is Psyche!

Now here is the ill hook to Didn't I Psyche Your Mind This Time and a mighty hook it is for the fooled:

> Psyche Yo Mind
> I
> Psyched Yo Mind
> Now ya sure nuff sinnin'
> all da time...
> Soon will see
> yo' soul
> in Hell
> with mine

MENTOR'S MISSION FUEL
A LETTER FROM A FAKE FRIEND

I am so proud of how you are ruining your life. You have taken some very important steps toward being nobody but it is my job to remind you that you still have a way to go before you are totally lost. So here are some tips to bring you beyond the point of no return. If you are serious about destroying your future, please pay close attention. My stuff works because I have mastered making self-destruction look like fun.

1. Pay no attention to the people you are hurting, especially your mother. Mothers have a powerful way of loving their children even when their children stop loving them. If you are not careful her love will get to you and you will stop destroying yourself. Why waste all of your wasted effort? When your mother is crying you make her cry more by ignoring her tears or acting like so what's the big deal. When she tries to reason with you say things that sound like you are sorry. It may make your mom or any other person that loves you think you have finally changed for the better. They will soon see that you ain't changed. You got worse. Oh how I love this deceptive work.

2. Keep hanging out with nobodies that are not going anywhere. Please know you can be the biggest nobody

in the bunch by letting go of all that you have been taught. Even though you probably will never see your present friends in the next couple of years because some will move, some will get busted; some will die and some, I have to admit, even though it kills me, will change their lives before it is too late. Make double sure you stay away from them because they learned the secret to resisting me. I had them in the same head lock I have you in and they got away.

3. Whatever you do please keep on getting high. In order to be a Class A nobody, you have to be low... I mean high all the time - that slipped. Don't pay attention to all of the drugged out nobodies you may see. That won't happen to you because you are different from them until you become the same as them. After all what's the big deal...you ain't hurtin' anybody in your desire to be nobody except for the people that care about you. Who needs them? You are grown so if you want nothing out of life that is your right to have all the nothing you can or can't handle. So puff on, snort on, shoot on, drink on, huff on until you can't remember that you once had dreams, that you were once loved, that you were not made to live the way you are living.

4. Speaking of forgetting. Forget about school... that ain't for you. What do you need school for if you are going to

be a big nobody? School is for people going somewhere. School is for people who think that just because they got an education that they have the right to be somebody in life. I love to make fun of people who go to school because their life can be so different than the life of my people. And if your path to nowhere happens to give you time for someone special in your life please make sure that you choose another nobody. Nothing worse than having another person who cares for you nagging you about changing your life, to stop hangin' out. My God. Did I say God? OOOOPPPS MY BAD. So keep on lowering your I.Q. till you start thinking to be smart is to be dumb and to be dumb is to be smart. Works every time!

5. And last, under no circumstance should you ever wonder if you should stop destroying yourself. Hell, you came this far, you may as well go all the way. And most important never, never under any circumstance close your eyes and pray. I never want you to know that your life can change by one honest prayer.

Well I have to go on my way to and fro, seeking whom I may destroy. My work on you my friend is just about complete. I had to write you this letter because there still are some folk, mainly your mother trying to convince other people that your life is not hopeless. I hate her because she never gives up. Can you believe she has found some man she wants to mentor you? If he calls, disguise your voice or just hang up the phone before he can start putting crazy notions in your head that you can do better. I can't believe she found a man through a mentoring program to help her help you. I have to step up my plan of discouragement on men before more start mentoring. I want you to hate him too. I have to send another imp to mess with him and his family so he will breakdown before he breaks through.

So keep on having fun tearing down your future by destroying your present. Don't worry about your dreams they will soon turn into a living nightmare when you realize that you did not have to end up doing time in a lock up (you are headed straight there to yet another nightmare, this time with bars!). All of the people under my control are losing themselves to utter and complete darkness. By the way it is getting dimmer and dimmer for you, but not to worry, where you are headed, you won't need light.

Signed

Bel Z. Bubb Your Worst Best Friend

MENTOR'S TESTIMONY

MY MENTOR MY DAD

By Chris Broussard

Chris Broussard is a sports analyst for ESPN, who mainly covers the NBA. He also is a columnist for ESPN Magazine and

ESPN.com. Broussard also makes appearances on ESPN's NBA Fastbreak as an analyst. Broussard graduated from Oberlin College in Ohio with a Bachelor's degree in English. In 1990, Broussard began his sports writing career for The Plain Dealer (Cleveland, Ohio). While a columnist for the Plain Dealer, Broussard was awarded the Ohio AP Sportswriters Award for General Excellence (1996), and the Ohio Excellence in Journalism Award (1998). He worked there for four years before moving to the Akron Beacon Journal where he started covering the NBA, spending two-and-a-half seasons with them as the Cleveland Cavaliers beat writer. Broussard then went on to work for The New York Times and began reporting for the New York Knicks and the New Jersey Nets. He started making a name for himself as one of the country's best sportswriter. He covered the New Jersey Nets for three years, the New York Knicks for two years, and the NBA in general for one year. In September 2004 Broussard joined ESPN Magazine. Since 2004, in addition to his writing duties, Broussard has also been seen frequently on ESPN as an NBA insider and analyst, and occasionally as a panelist on First Take debating sports topics. Aside from writing for ESPN Magazine and appearing on ESPN programs, Broussard also found the time to write for such publications as The Source Magazine, The Source Sports Magazine, Athlon Sports Magazine, Courtside Magazine, Hoop Magazine, Magic Basket Magazine He also wrote the non-fiction novel "Not Without Scars: The Inspiring Life Journey of Mark C. Olds". Broussard is married to Crystal Naii Collins Broussard

My mentor growing up was the man who ideally would be every boy's mentor - dad. I never needed a "mentor" in the sense that the word is used today because my father, Ed Broussard, was always there. He wasn't perfect and I witnessed some of his flaws, but my love and respect for him never wavered. Not once. And I believe that's in part because again, he was there. Fathers need to realize that part of the job description is being there. I understand that stuff happens and sometimes it's not possible for fathers to live with their children, but know this: it will be hard to meet your child's emotional needs if you don't see them on what is essentially a daily basis. Even if you're a good and dedicated father, if you only see your child every couple of weeks, you're more likely to end up being the equivalent of an uncle or a big brother. It's hard to have the authority a father is supposed to have with his children when you're not there just about every day.

Ed Broussard was there. He was there when I learned how to ride a bike. He was there when I played my first tee-ball game. He coached me in my first football game, and took me to Johnny Bench's Home Plate restaurant when I got straight A's in the second grade. I could go on - my first communion, my first fight, my first date, my first job, my Senior Prom. Dad was always there. We watched games on television together. He helped me with my homework. He taught me how to box and cut the grass and rake the leaves and shovel the snow. The lessons I learned from my father weren't always verbal lessons. In fact, more often than not, I just picked things up from him by being around him. But that was only possible because he was there always there.

My father taught me how to respect authority, most importantly his. And he taught me that a man's first priority is to take care of his family. We moved to six different cities from the time I was born to the time I finished high school because my father's job transferred him. He left great friends and houses and communities, not always because he wanted to, but because that's what was necessary to take care of his wife and kids. If it meant cramping his lifestyle or causing him pain then so be it: he was a man and his duty was to provide. That's what I learned from my mentor, my dad.

MENTOR'S TESTIMONY
WHEN THE STREETS CALL
By Charles Dotson III

For over twenty years, Charles Dotson III has counseled and trained a diverse population of clients with the goal of helping them achieve personal growth and to improve overall social functioning. Over the course of his career, he has supervised clients consisting of men and women, who have abused drugs, have had patterns of impulsive, angry behaviors, were involved in gangs, or participated in gang related activities. A number of these clients were deemed "high profile" due to the nature of their crime. Raised in New York, the importance of education, church, and community service were instilled in him at an early age through his sound family background. Living to help others stabilize their home and personal life continues to cement the values of his youth. Mr. Dotson's strong focus, determination, and passion for knowledge, led him to graduate from the State University of New York at New Paltz with a Bachelor's Degree in African-American Studies and from Marist College where he obtained a Master's Degree in Public Administration. Mr. Dotson has worked in minimum and maximum security juvenile detention facilities in New York State. He also has twelve years of experience as a Federal Law Enforcement Officer (This essay was written from the time when Bro. Dotson was a federal probation officer), five years of experience providing intensive home-based family therapy to court adjudicated youth and is currently employed as a Program Director of a mentoring program working with young adult probationers. His distinguished career has allowed him to specialize in working with drug offenders, organized crime groups, and criminal enterprise members. Mr. Dotson is considered an expert in the area of street gangs. Mr. Dotson is a father and respected community leader.

I met Mike in 2001 after he served seven years in the Federal Bureau of Prisons for "Conspiracy to Distribute Crack Cocaine." Mike "hustled" during the "glory days" of drug dealing in an era when drug dealers accumulated an abundance of income peddling poison in the community. He was a member of an organization that distributed crack for a notorious dealer in Harlem whose story is chronicled in the classic "hood" film *Paid in Full*. It was not hard to recognize that Mike was different from typical drug dealers. Not only was he built like a linebacker, he was charming, personable, charismatic and blessed with the "gift of gab." While Mike "did time" in the Bureau of Prisons, he did not waste time. During his sentence he enrolled in a

Personal Fitness Trainer course offered by the Department of Justice's Occupational Training Program. After his release from custody, with a body sculpted like a superhero, he descended on the streets of Manhattan determined and prepared to land a lucrative job as a personal trainer.

Unlike most new releasees from prison, Mike had a strong support system. His fiancée was a paralegal at a profitable law firm. She provided him positive feedback and support. I steadfastly encouraged him to focus on his career goals and refrain from socializing with peers who might lure him back to the streets. I would tell him, "When the streets call, don't pick up the phone." Mike quickly landed a job at a popular fitness gym in Manhattan. His physique and charming personality allowed him to attract and retain affluent clients. I would visit and applaud him for not only obtaining a job he enjoyed but one that paid him exceptionally well.

Mike was on a roll. His fiancée was beaming with joy. She was pleasantly surprised that he was fulfilling the promises that he made while he was in prison. He opened a bank account and was saving money which would allow them to purchase their first home. Their future was bright. Inspired by the prospects of their future, Mike and his fiancée began planning their wedding.

A year later, Mike started to accept calls from old acquaintances from his time on the street. He began interacting with these associates who were still "in the life" - selling drugs, gambling and frequenting strip clubs. He eventually began using drugs. I was concerned. I noticed a change in his appearance and whenever I questioned him about this he would smile dismissively and attempt to change the subject. I felt that with persistent effort, I would persuade him to level with me about the change I had noticed in him. One day his fiancée telephoned me. She said that Mike was working all week, however, on Fridays after getting paid, he would not come home. She expressed frustration over the situation and spoke of her desire to end the relationship. She was distraught and exclaimed, "I did not sign up for THIS!" I advised her that I could not guarantee that Mike would change. However, I assured her that I would confront him over these concerns in an effort to have him reconsider the direction his life was taking.

The next time I saw Mike we had a discussion about what he valued and loved. We conducted a cost/benefit analysis of everything that was transpiring in his life. Tearfully, he admitted that his job, his income, his fiancée, his freedom and his joy far outweighed life in the strip club and getting high. He also was determined to avoid re-entering a 6x8 jail cell. He asked me to assist him in entering an inpatient drug treatment program and requested my continued counseling and support. I agreed to continue to counsel him and he gradually regained his confidence.

Two years later I received a card from Mike that contained a wedding picture of him and his wife. In it, they thanked me for my advice, my encouragement, support and feedback during a difficult period in their lives. To me, mentoring is all about modeling, inspiring, encouraging, supporting and empowering. It is often difficult to help someone alter their maladaptive behavior patterns. However, a mentor can be a life jacket for someone who is drowning. A mentor plants seeds of wisdom that can mature into a mighty oak long after the formal mentoring relationship has ended.

CHAPTER ELEVEN

MENTOR'S LAMENT

My eyes fail from weepin,. I am in torment within, my heart is poured out on the ground because my people are destroyed, because children and infants faint in the streets of the city. Lamentations 2:11

While I have had success mentoring three generations of young people (the oldest are now in their 40's and 50's), I must confess that I have not always been a successful mentor. Despite my best intention my effort at times has met with failure. The residual feeling did not sit well with me. Mentors would like to save everyone, but that is not possible. It is difficult to sacrifice personal time and energy graciously extended to another person only to have this effort unappreciated. It is the rare helper that reoffers the proverbial apple knocked out of his hand. Failure can be demoralizing and have a negative impact on potential mentors standing on the sidelines. Any mentor that is honest must admit there will always be mentees that you cannot reach for whatever reason. It is important to not solely revel in what works in the mentoring process. It is equally important to study what did not work and make adjustments. Here are two examples of good intention/bad results stories.

Story # 1

I recall a harrowing event from a secular youth program I was affiliated with in the 80's. We were working with a large number of exceptionally challenged youth for the first time. Many were court adjudicated and most if not all were in foster care. As I was conducting the group orientation, a young man picked up a hammer from a nearby tool shed and started pounding the table as he menacingly glared at me. This was done in full view of about 35 other young people so it could not be ignored. The implied threat to me and to the safety of the other participants was unnerving. I had been challenged before but this was different - real different. I had to respond quickly and decisively or I would lose the respect and trust of the other students and thereby communicating your safety is your problem.

Drawing on years of experience, I knew that showing fear was the desired response 'Mr. Hammer' wanted. I slowly moved toward the young man and without missing a beat, as I was about to walk by, whispered in his ear that he should put the hammer down while I was talking. He was completely thrown off by the lack of emotion in my voice and thankfully he complied. I called his agency during a break and told them that he was discharged from the program because we did not have the skills to meet his needs. I still wonder what became of him. The takeaway from this story is that just because you want to help a young person does not always mean you can.

Story # 2

There was another young man in the same program as 'Mr. Hammer'. He was always cutting up. He was not threatening - just not serious. He was given many breaks by staff and would straighten up for a few days only to revert back to the same undisciplined behavior. After the pattern was set, and it was clear that the playful young man would not change, he was discharged from the program. It was my job to inform him he was no longer a part of the team. I took him off to the side and told him that we were not the right place for him and that it would be in his best interest to try another program if he still wanted to get his GED. He left yelling that he would get his GED and show us that we were wrong.

About two years later, I was riding the subway and heard a voice over the din of the moving train yelling, "I told you. I told you." When I was able to locate the shouter, much to my surprise it was the young man I terminated from the program. He was not angrily shouting but it was excitement that caused his voice to rise. He said, "I told you, I told you I would get my GED and I did!" I smiled and hugged him. The takeaway from this story is that my perceived failure was another mentor's success.

Mentor/mentee matching is more than looking around a room and pairing folk up much like how we used to choose sides in a pick-up basketball game. The easy way to explain a bad mentor/mentee pairing is to entirely focus on and ultimately blame the young person and pay scant attention to what role the mentor may have played in the failed relationship. Here are some thoughts on how it is possible to have the best mentoring intentions and yet there is a bad mentoring result:

- **Mentor/Mentee Mismatch**—Just because you want to help does not always mean you will be helpful. There is a certain chemistry that must exist between the mentor and the mentee that takes time, conversation and conscious relationship building to develop. This is the 'get to know you' phase that all relationships require. After time has passed (it varies according to the pairing) and it becomes clear that the chemistry is nonexistent then chances are the match will not take.

- **Mentor/Mentee Is Not Ready To Change—** It is difficult to help a person change if the person either is not ready to change or refuses to change. This may be hard to accept especially if the mentor is convinced that the young person must change because the present behavior, if continued, will threaten his future. Remember this simple postulate: Whenever you want success for a person more than the person wants for himself it will always be the deeper aspirant who is disappointed if change does not occur

- **Mentor/Mentee Relationship Is One-Sided—**If one person is always giving or always taking there is no room for real sharing. A mentor must know when to lead, when to guide, when to talk, when to listen and when silence can be beneficial. It is easy for an adult to look at their accomplishments and earned life wisdom and think it is their job to impart this knowledge and experience at every turn. Unfortunately, when this happens, the young person's real needs may not be met. One of the great skills of a mentor is learning how to listen.

- **Mentor/Mentee Competitiveness**—It is one thing to be competitive, most males are. It is another thing to consistently place winning above understanding in any relationship. When winning becomes more important than understanding the benefits of mentoring will ultimately be lost in a game of one-upmanship. A man that must win every interaction no matter the cost is a danger to the mentee, the program and to himself.

- **Mentor/Mentee Unbalanced Context**--It has been proven that mentoring is helpful on multiple levels for the mentor and mentee. Yet it is important to look past the obvious i.e. a boy needs a man in his life or that a man should want to be a mentor. It is imperative to set a structured, consistent mentoring context with ongoing training, assessment, orientation and evaluation for mentors and mentees. This includes supportive parents and informed and engaged leadership.

- **Mentor/Mentee Dual Lack**—It may be clear when a young person is in need of a mentor, what is not always clear is when the mentor needs a mentor. It is difficult to find men willing to become mentors and it is sometimes difficult to admit that a man is not ready to mentor. After all an empty vessel cannot replenish an empty vessel, no way, no how, no kidding.

Questions to Ponder

1. Can you cite an example when you were not able to help a person change his situation in spite of your best effort?

2. Can you recall someone trying to help turn your life around and you were not ready to receive their help?

3. What are other "blocks" that can get in the way of developing a dynamic and transformative mentoring relationship?

MENTOR'S SPIRITUAL REFLECTION
MAN UP!

When I was a child, I talked like a child, I thought like a child, I reasoned like a child. When I became a man, I put childish ways behind me. 1Corinthians 13:11

In order to Man Up you have to commit to growing up. It is disturbing to either be, or witness a grown man shackled to his adolescent state of being and mindset. I am not talking about men who experience what is called mid-life crisis. I am talking about men who refuse to mature; who refuse to accept responsibility for thought, word or deed; men who hurt people (children) that love them because they are more in love with people, places and things that please their flesh and assuage their stunted ego. It is clear that some men benefit by being perpetual boys (Peter Pan Syndrome). These boy/men in love with playing (playaz) will find ever creative ways and excuses to refuse to Man Up.

Some men cannot find the words to say, 'I need help. I want to Man Up, but I don't know how.' These brothers should not to be rejected or ridiculed because it is hard for a man to be vulnerable to self or others. Some brothers are not open to discussing their past either out of embarrassment or worse, because of a comforting feeling of self-righteousness. Men we have to tell our story to young men and to each other. My brother, will you tell how you handled: family responsibilities, peer pressure while growing up, racism, sexual temptation, adversity, personal issues? Will you shed light on how you climbed the rungs of the manhood ladder? You know how males of all ages are, so please do not tear down a brother in a vain attempt to build him up. If a man feels attacked he will most certainly defend.

I recall a conversation I had with a young man in his 30's whom I have known since he was a child. I assumed he had general questions about life and what it meant to be a man. I successfully engaged him in a Man Up conversation by talking about my early missteps, setbacks and hard learned man lessons. Up to this point all he knew about me was that I was the son of his pastor, a successful, college educated black man with national reach and deep hook-ups. After I shared the real me inside of me, he in turn felt comfortable to open up and ask for personal direction. The cry to Man Up is readily embraced when it is used as a macho call to action. However, it is easy to ignore when linked to fessing up. My brother it is time to Man Up!

Questions To Ponder

1. Can you recall an event or time in your life when you had to Man Up?
2. Why do you think some men in and out of the church refuse to Man Up?
3. What man in reality or fiction best captures your concept of a real man?

MENTOR'S MISSION FUEL
BOUNCE BACK DAD AWARDS

One does not have to be a social scientist to know that many young men are being raised in homes with absent fathers. I have been involved in Men's ministry for several decades and it never ceases to amaze me how many men, regardless of their age, have grown up without a consistent father presence. It is ironic that some of these same men opt to become mentors. This is not to say that fatherless men cannot successfully mentor fatherless youth. What this observation may suggest is that some mentors without dads feel a sense of urgency to fill the fatherless void in others. There are some 'no matter what' fathers who stalwartly weather life's storms; these brothers refuse to give up, give in or run away from their responsibility or a need.

So much has been written about the family and community impact of fathers who are present and as well as absentee fathers. Lost in mounting bad news and broken relationships are strong brothers refusing to become a negative statistic. If you have complained that you do not hear positive stories about people of color in general, or men in particular, I have good news for you. In a proactive effort to honor men (of all ages) who are doing the right thing, I hereby authorized the creation of the Bounce Back Dad Award (BBDA) recognizing poppa excellence under pressure. You don't have to wait for media outlets to find committed fathers. Feel free to recognize men of all ages who are exemplars of fatherhood. Here are sample categories to get you started.

Returning Fathers/Fathers Behind Bars

For the last five years or so, I have been privileged to be the keynote speaker for the Osborne Association's (I am a Board member) Family Works Prison Program at Sing-Sing Prison. This program was once run by a colleague and friend Dr. Carl Mazza. He taught parenting skills to incarcerated men (some will never be released). I have the utmost respect for brothers who graduate from this program. This category of BBDA recognizes men in prison and men who have returned from prison, rehab, shelters or other adverse situations to play an integral, consistent and healthy role in their family.

Single Fathers

There are single fathers who are raising their children. These dads may have lost the mother of their children to death, divorce, or a breakup. Whatever the situation, these men did the right thing by ensuring the best for their family evidenced by their physical, emotional, spiritual and financial support of their children. While there are far less single fathers than single mothers, it is important to give a shout out of encouragement to brothers who did not run away or move on to the next situation (woman) with little or no concern for their children left behind.

Community Fathers

(Special Mention Category)

To all of the men who may not have children but have raised children as surrogate fathers, foster dads, godfathers, mentors, scout masters, role models and the like this category is dedicated to you. A community father is a person who steps up to provide male energy, support and guiding presence in the life of a child, young adult or grown man. I am working in partnership with New York City's Administration for Children's Service (ACS) in an effort to match mentors with young people who have aged out of the child welfare system. There are youth programs across the country looking for caring men capable of playing a positive role in the healthy development of a young person.

Good community parents can make a significant life-changing difference just like good parents.

Fathers Without Fathers

I meet men of all ages who have never experienced a father's consistent presence while growing up. Some of these brothers go on to become fathers while secretly yearning for a daddy blueprint. I want to recognize brothers who did not have a father in the house but found the wherewithal to not repeat the absent dad syndrome. So much attention is placed on the negative impact and drama caused by absent fathers, that it is important to counterbalance this news by recognizing strong brothers who have successfully broken the bad dad cycle. It is prudent at this juncture to recognize mothers who had to be fathers to their children. If it were not for strong women playing all the roles a child needs to grow and develop, our families would be in far worse shape.

Elder Dads

In this youth orientated culture, it is so easy to forget the importance of elders. I want to recognize fathers who have grown children, grandchildren and perhaps great grandchildren. Elder dads, please hear this: life is not over. You may not have the same get up and go; you may not be able to move around as freely as you wish, but don't give up. Your family and community still need you. What you know about being a family man is not tied to being current or socially connected. There are some lessons that will always be true. What is true is that you raised and launched your children's careers. What is true is that you weathered life's storm, learned lessons and have earned valuable wisdom. Can we give a big hug, cheer and standing ovation for the elder dads in the community?

Beloved, you have been instructed and now encouraged to be persistent and resilient in creating your own BBDA effort particular to your community and resources. The more fathers that can be officially recognized the more families who can be reached and helped.

A MENTOR'S TESTIMONY
A GRATEFUL, SON, FATHER AND HUSBAND
By Greg Owens LMSW

Greg Owens is a husband, father and faithful member of Macedonia Baptist Church in Albany, NY. He works for the New York State Office of Children and Family Services. Bro Greg is a national leader addressing the needs of court adjudicated and incarcerated juveniles. One of his specialty areas is disproportionality-looking at the overrepresentation of children of color in juvenile detention facilities. He is a licensed social worker with over 30 years of experience. He is an accomplished singer, a former jazz DJ on the radio and volunteer track and field coach.

We just returned from my father-in-law's home going celebration this weekend in South Jersey. Pop Green was one of those rare men who changed the environment around him, not by what he said but rather by what he did. He could have held any office in the city of Paulsboro, New Jersey, but he chose to remain a humble servant, a father to his daughter, my beloved wife, a pillar of strength, wisdom and love to our 15-year-old daughter, and a devoted husband.

Thinking of him makes me think of my father. In many ways, he was very much like my father-in-law. From humble beginnings in Decatur, Alabama, my dad became one of the first Black dentists in Westchester. Despite coming from a single parent home, he excelled in school, served in the Air Force, and married my mother with whom he remained devoted until the Lord took him home in 2005. They had 3 children, and I am the middle child. Hearing that may help make sense of what follows.

My most profound mentoring memory is when my Dad saved the house from burning down when I set the bed on fire! Understand that I was an inquisitive, young, middle child, and always into something. I was the adventurous one, who took the risks, and often paid the price. So one day playing around with matches, I set my parents bed on fire... My Mom and I were running around, throwing burning pillows out of the windows and calling to our next door neighbor for help.

I looked out of the 2nd floor window and saw my Dad's car come up the hill. He jumped out, appeared in the bedroom as if by magic, told me to get out of the way, rolled up the mattress, pushed it out of the window, and on to the front steps. Soon the fire department arrived, sprayed the room to make sure that the fire was entirely out and the officer then approached my father.

Upon discovering that I had started it, he informed my Dad that he would have to take me with him. I was about 10 at the time, and those words frightened me beyond measure. I knew that I was in trouble, but the idea that I could be arrested was so foreign to me, so bizarre, that I almost passed out. Then I heard my father say, "No, I'll handle this." There was more conversation between them, but what I remember is that moment, when I knew that I was saved.

Later, my dad showed me the damage and said, "Take a look at what you have done, son. Now go to your room, because if you don't, I might hurt you." Over the next few weeks, he took me with him as he searched for a new bed. Because he was well known, he was often stopped by patients and friends. He let them know that he was shopping for a new bed set because his son had set the other one on fire. I tried to hide in the well of the space between the front and back seats, but the public shame and humiliation were inescapable. In retrospect, it was a small price to pay.

My Dad was a hero, not just because he arrived like an angel in time to save us, not just because of his Sampson like strength that enabled him to fold a queen size mattress in half and push it out of the window, but because he saved me from those who were going to take me away, and later he forgave me. He never stopped loving me, even though he was very disappointed in me and what I had done.

This is what unreserved love is, and I was blessed to learn it at an early age, from the person that God placed on this earth to teach it to me. This is the strength of fathers, who are also mentors, and who teach their children about love, redemption, accountability and forgiveness. I wish that I could say that this was the last time that I did something crazy, but it was not the last time that my parents, and especially my father, forgave me.

So thank you Dad and Mom, my first and greatest mentors! Humbly Submitted by a Grateful Son, Father and Husband!

Questions to Ponder

1. What memories do you have of your father?

2. Is there a man in your life, past or present, who did not birth you but is like a father to you? Who is he and describe the relationship?

3. If you could go back in time and address a father issue what would you want to rectify?

MENTOR'S MISSION FUEL
10 WAYS TO PUT YOURSELF SECOND
By Mark Merrill

The following essay was taken from Family First/ All Pro Dad website.

Mark Merrill is founder and president of Family First an organization with a mission to strengthen the family by establishing family as a top priority in people's lives and by promoting principles for building marriages and raising children. Family First has joined with Hall of Fame football coach Tony Dungy to create All Pro Dad. The following was taken from Mark Merrill's website.

Second? What? Our culture does not teach us to strive for second. We are in unchartered waters here. People advocate for you to find ways to put yourself first, to make more money, to do a myriad of things, but nobody out there is telling you to come in second. The dictionary defines the word second when used as an adjective as "being the latter of two equal parts." That is a good way to look at things. Not less than anyone else, because we are not, but supportive and mindful of the needs of the people around us first. Is it not the duty of a man to do exactly this for his wife and family? Aren't the best leaders the type of people who share the sacrifice and shoulder the load for others to move forward?

Millions of people daily ask the question "what is love?" One thing love surely must be is selfless. No marriage ever winds up in couples therapy because the relationship is not selfish enough. Family problems occur and family relationships wind up in peril because individuals pursue their own desires in life and not the needs of the entire group. Here are a few ideas to consider as you place yourself on the path to second place.

1. **Visualize Yourself Less Selfish**

   The more selfish you are, the less you realize it (or care). Start with knowing you are pretty self-centered and visualize yourself being less so. Just like anything else, if you strive to be something, it takes training and practice. Over time those other-centered traits will become habits and eventually you will be less about yourself. A man wrapped up in himself is a very small package.

2. **Consider What the Other Person Is Going Through**

   The annoyances in life can be so frustrating. Like when we get cut off in traffic on our way home from work. We cringe when we get stuck behind the person with 18 items in the 10 items only lane at the grocery store. How about the van in the drive-thru ordering for 10 people instead of going inside to do it? The list is nearly endless. These annoyances usually draw our most fiery reactions and wrath. How dare this person inconvenience me! But what are they going through that might be causing them to act so thoughtlessly? Putting ourselves second in those situations will not only greatly reduce our stress levels; it will also help open our eyes to the suffering of others. Instead of being blinded by rage, our eyes may instead notice that the extra items at the grocery store are medical items for a sick child at home. Or the man who cut us off in traffic feels disgusting because he just came from a chemo treatment. We just never know...

3. **Display Unexpected Kindness**

Many people feel like it is them against the world. As Norm from *Cheers* once famously said, "It's a dog-eat-dog world and I'm wearing Milk Bone underwear." How many circumstances do we hear and see where people completely disregard the well-being of others? We watch the crazed shoppers pushing in a store for sale items while they step over the elderly man on the floor in cardiac arrest and gasping for air. Are you the person who would keep going for the 50% off television? Or are you the rare exception who would help the man to safety and get him medical attention? Your superficial needs sacrificed for the real life and death need of a fellow human being. Practice displaying unexpected kindness in your interactions with people. It is not too simple to say that sometimes just a genuine smile can make all the difference in the world in the day of someone else.

4. **Avoid the At All Costs Mentality**

"Get it done at all costs!" We have all heard that at some point in our lives, and some hear it every single day. It is said to inspire laser-type focus and motivation. But the actual "costs" are not often considered. Those costs are destructive and damaging to an overall larger plan. If times are desperate enough to call for such action, then it is time for wiser, calmer heads to consider other alternatives. Place yourself second in these situations and actually consider what the costs really are. Are they worth the short-term gain?

5. **Take What You Need and Leave the Rest**

We are a consumer society. We do it quite well. We have two and three of just about everything. "Take what you need and leave the rest" is a value that seems foreign to a lot of us now. However, if we returned to such a simple principle of a decent society, how much better could the world be for all of its inhabitants? Strive to be second, consume less, and prize the rare jewel of contentment.

6. **Leave Judgment to God**

How much of our lives do we waste brooding over useless grudges and dreams of judgment and revenge? These thoughts literally eat our own insides away while the object of our scorn usually is clueless to our hidden desires. Let these things go. They are the height of self-centeredness. Have we not done worse to others? By letting go of the destructive feelings harboring inside of us, we put ourselves second by letting God handle these hurts first.

7. **Practice Healthy Habits**

This might seem like a self-centered suggestion. It isn't when one considers the ramifications our health has on the people that count on us the most. Our wives, our children, our friends and our business partners depend on us daily. That requires we strive to be healthy and clear thinking as much as possible. This is one we probably all need to really work on, because it is easy to consider health our own business. Usually it is not until tragedy occurs that the wake-up call is received. Let us place ourselves second behind the needs of those who dearly count on us and love us. They need us here for as long as possible, so let's have the discipline to be healthy.

8. **Master Invisible Leadership**

If glory and fame are your ambition, then this is a worthless strategy. If the idea instead is to esteem others better than yourself, then there is no better way to lead than to be practically invisible. It takes a selfless ego and great skill to be humble. This is basically the "man behind the curtain" theory, except used for positive results. There is great satisfaction to be found in watching a plant blossom from afar. Knowing that it is not tainted by any elements of greed or desire, but just pure and of decent intent. Master the art of invisible leadership.

9. **Envy Is For the Weak**

No matter our station in life, there will always be another that has topped us in some form or fashion. Chasing after the hope that somehow you wind up at the very top of the pyramid is just a fool's desire. What is so great once you get there? Nothing. Just the constant fear of being knocked off now that you've made it. Envy leads to these types of pointless, self-involved adventures. "If a man gains the whole world, but loses his soul, what did he gain?" Leave envy for the losers. In the end, it all goes back in the box. Realize what truly matter is what survives your death.

10. **Build a Wealthy Spirit**

Ask any human on their deathbed what true wealth is, and they will undoubtedly tell you that it has zero to do with monetary stature. True wealth is accumulated by doing exactly what this list is preaching, and that is putting ourselves second as much as we can. Kindness, sympathy, compassion, hard work, honesty and sincerity are but a few of the key ingredients to a selfless, extremely rich existence. Live well. Live second.

I met Brother Darrin Gray, Director of Corporate Partnerships for All Pro Dad while on a 'Rumble Young Man Rumble' retreat at The Muhammad Ali Center in Louisville, Kentucky. I told him that I spoke at an All Pro Dad event a year earlier and while I did not know the genesis of All Pro Dad at the time, I could not deny the power of seeing fathers in school on a weekday afternoon participating in the lives of their children. As God would have it, a year later, I was asked by Darrin Gray to work with Tony Dungy and All Pro Dad.

Here are 10 Ways To Be An All Pro Dad.

1. Love your wife

2. Spend time with your children

3. Be a role model

4. Understand your children

5. Show affection

6. Enjoy your children

7. Eat together as a family

8. Discipline with a gentle spirit

9. Pray and worship together

10. Realize you are a father forever

For more information about All Pro Dad go to www.AllProDad.com

CHAPTER TWELVE

MENTORING IN CHALLENGING TIMES

*He who is in you is greater than he who is in the world.
They are in the world. Therefore they speak as of the world,
and the world hears them. We are of God. He who knows
God hears us; he who is not of God does not hear us. By
this we know the spirit of truth and the spirit of error.
1John 4: 4b-6 (NKJV)*

The devastation to families caused by Crack, missing fathers, the preponderance of single-parent-headed households generational poverty, gangs; the over-incarceration of people of color, has made mentoring even more challenging as it is needed. Add to these very real problems the ascendancy of the world's unholy trinity: *Crude, Lewd and Rude* and a disturbing societal view that further exacerbates the task of developing young people through mentoring comes into focus.

The Crude, Lewd and Rude reality is spread by young and not-so-young multimillionaire toxic icons strolling down the coveted red carpet of The Grammy's, MTV, BET or other music award shows. Their target is the impressionable youth/young adult demographic to sell their products and lifestyle. Negative icons have penetrated and taken residence in the heart, mind and spirit of young men to the degree that we have a generation of voyeuristic "gangsta wannabes" who are convinced that this is a viable and profitable way to live. The 'Thug For Life' philosophy is still alive and well. Unfortunately this thinking is largely played out in jails and prisons across the country.

It is easy for adults to say that young people of the present generation are worse than previous generations. The reality is that each generation of youth gets this tag. Look back to when you were young. When you thought you knew everything about everything. When you felt adults were nothing more than clueless 'groove knockers' trying to ruin your fun with an endless list of rules and regulations. Think back to your music, red light parties, at-risk behavior that could have landed you in trouble - or got you in trouble. It is plain to see that each generation was thought to be the bane of adults. It is advisable to carry the memory of how you felt growing up and how you related to adults while you are currently mentoring.

This simple act can help you to not personalize your interaction with your young charge. Your mentee may very well remind you of you, but please remember he is not you! Over-identification with a mentee can be as harmful as having no basis for identification. If you gloss over or constantly excuse potentially destructive behavior exhibited by your mentee because it conjures up behavior you exhibited when you were young, please know that you are enabling harmful patterns that if unchecked can have deleterious consequences. The adversary's job is to make self-destruction look like fun. The mentor's challenge is to find ways to unmask the deceiver and his plan to steal, kill, rob and destroy God's creation. Mentors, please share how you got out of the grips of self-destruction. How you solved vexing life problems. How you overcame a problematic obstacle in life when you were at or near the same age of your mentee.

If you have a choice between talking about how you forestalled foreclosure (which may be a great story to tell) or how you evaded joining a gang the latter may be more relevant to the young person still living at home and not paying a mortgage. Please, however, don't glory in your past, but extract powerful lessons from your experiences and then pass it along. After you share then actively listen. One of the accusations that young people make against adults is that all they want to do is be in charge and get their 'stuff' off. One of the ways to deconstruct the enemy's mission is through active listening and sharing. When you listen, you learn and when you learn you grow. When a mentor and a mentee are simultaneously listening and sharing the basis for a transformative relationship is developed.

Case Study On Listening And Sharing

Some years ago I recall leading a discussion on a men's retreat (young people were included for the first time). I told the men that we would not beat up on the seven youth in attendance. I had to repeat several times that I would stop any attacks on the young people. It took 45 minutes of stops and starts before the men saw that I was serious. Once I was able to move forward my first question to the men was, "How many of you had to walk through metal detectors when you were in school?" No hands were raised. I asked the same question to the teens and all of their hands shot up. In between the void created by these two questions was the meat we needed to chew. One of the young men talked about his fear of going to school because while there were metal detectors, it was nothing for someone to open a back door and weapons could be slipped into the school. The father of the young man who shared this with the group stood up. He was in tears. He walked over to his son and put his arm around him and said, "All this time I thought you did not want to go to school because you were lazy. I had no idea that you were afraid." They both cried as they left the circle and went up to their room.

Questions To Ponder

1. What similarities and differences can you present concerning the time you grew up and the time that young people are growing up?

2. If you had a "do over" in life what one thing would you want to change?

3. Can you give an example when your ability to share and/or listen was useful in addressing an important issue?

MENTOR'S SPIRITUAL REFLECTION
MEN FACE YOUR FEARS: A WORD OF ENCOURAGEMENT
2Kings 6: 8-17

The biblical story deals with a subject many men are reluctant to share. I am talking about the things that keep you up at night. I am referring to that secret torment stemming from looking like you got it together on the outside, but you are slowly unraveling on the inside. My brothers I have a word of liberation, a word of elevation, a word of encouragement, so that you may be free, like David, to encourage yourself so that you may encourage others. My assigned word is: Men It is Time To Face Your Fears.

The first thought that may have zoomed into your mind is the preacher surely is not talking to me. I don't have fears. I am a real man and real men don't cry. A real man does not worry. A real man will never let others see him sweat. I fully understand this macho 'I can't be hurt thinking.' As a man we are conditioned by society to not deal with feelings. This is why some brothers have tremendous difficulty acknowledging or facing their fears.

Let's go to the text and see what we can learn about facing one's fears.

We find that Israel no longer heeds the word of God. The chosen people have made another choice. They want to be like the people around them and opt to be ruled by kings instead of The King of Kings. They did not want Yahweh but wanted their way. God sent the prophets to warn the people to turn from their apostasy. The people lost the fear of God and continued to sin. We read that an army of Assyrians were about to descend on Israel. The king of the invaders is trying to figure out who is tipping off the King of Israel's troops.

Whatever strategic move he makes, the army of Israel knows in advance before the move is made. The Assyrian king is informed that there is a prophet named Elisha (God Delivers) who is probably the cause of the security leak. The king decides to send an army of 50,000 men to subdue this loose-lipped prophet and simultaneously plug this security breach.

The Bible tells us that early in the morning Elisha's servant arose and discovered that the Assyrian army surrounded the city. The servant, stricken with fear, runs to Elisha shouting, "Oh my Lord what shall we do?" Fear will make you panic. Fear makes you feel vulnerable, helpless, unworthy and uncared for. Fear can force you to make bad decisions, say things you don't really mean. Fear can make you hurt yourself and others. The Prophet Elisha was special. He listened to his servant. He did not ignore him. He did not laugh at him for being afraid.

He did not say, 'handle your 'bizzniss' like a man...' 'The Bible says that Elisha encouraged the young man. This is the way Elisha did it. He addressed the young man's fear directly. He said, "Fear not because those who are with us are more than those who are with them." It did not end there. Elisha encouraged the young servant not by recounting manly stories of his triumph over insurmountable odds or by using a Knute Rockne inspired expression like, "When the going gets tough the tough get going."

My Bible tells me that Elisha prayed a specific prayer. He pleaded to God, "Open the servant's eyes so that he might see." We are told that the young man looked a second time at the same trouble and now saw chariots of fire ringed around Elisha. Yes, the enemy had chariots but no consuming fire. The Lord can reveal his power in the most challenging situations. The limit of one's ability to address a pressing problem or situation is the beginning of fear and an opportunity to embrace God. Elisha gave his mentee confidence on several levels. He stood by his servant (presence). He spoke to the problem at hand (focused). He prayed a specific prayer (strategic). Brothers always remember:

For God did not give us a spirit of fear, but of power and of love and of a sound mind 1Timothy1:7

MENTOR'S MISSION FUEL
FEARS OF MEN CULLED FROM VARIOUS RETREATS/WORKSHOPS

I have been asked by churches to conduct workshops or facilitate retreats for men. It is not easy getting men to open up for reasons already mentioned. Most men are of the mindset that their fears are their business. Some can press on and others are crushed by fear. Fear has torment. Fear can immobilize you. Fear can make you believe the unbelievable. Fear can marginalize you. Fear can make you sick. Fear can drive you to drink. Fear can enrage you. Fear can oppress, compress, stress and depress you. Look at the word fear: **False Evidence Appearing Real.** Fear lives in the mind and invades the whole being.

So here is a list of unedited fears that were offered by brothers of varying ages and length of church membership. Many were on retreat or participating in a workshop of this nature for the first time.

- My fear of trusting or depending on others for help and that I will get old and retire in poverty, being a disappointment to my family.

- Fear of rejection when I <u>want</u> to share things with my wife.

- Fear of submitting my total self to God because of my comfort zone of knowing that I am in control.

- How God will use me and whether I will be able to do more.

- Fear of being single for the rest of my life.

- I worry about not being able to do God's work when He calls.

- Fear of my mother dying and [fear of] my kid being fatherless.

- I will miss God's will or His calling.

- Fear of being one paycheck away from being homeless and failing health.

- My fear is disobeying God

- My fear is that I fear sickness. I am going [through] that right now.

- Being locked up.

- Fear of being unemployed and unable to provide for my family.

- Studying God's Word/speaking God's Word.

- Doing the right thing/ helping our men more.

- Stepping forward and taking charge.

- Fear of my [lack of] school education.

- My spelling hold [sic] me back from getting ahead.

- I'm up in age at this time, but I [fear] for my children. I pray that my children will continue to [obey]. I continue to pray for them at all times.

- At this time, my worse fear is for my daughter the way her life in her marriage [turned out]. Please pray for this marriage and my daughter.

- Let my family receive the Word of God through attachment in each other. I will help them reach their goal with the help of my brothers in the ministry.

- I am looking forward to being a good follower so that I can eventually be a good disciple.

- I am concerned about my sister who has not accepted Jesus The Christ. I am not sure what to say to her because she is bitter and depressed and I don't always know what to say to people.

- My fears are that my health will fail and I won't be able to take care of myself; or that my mind might be affected in a way that I might not be able to think properly.

- I fear what might happen if we go to war; what will the consequences be?

MENTOR'S TESTIMONY
IT'S NEVER TOO LATE
By Gerald Bell

Gerald has been Communications Manager for the DeVos Urban Leadership Initiative since 2004. He serves as city liaison to Cleveland, Denver, Detroit, Kansas City, Los Angeles and Pittsburgh. Gerald enjoys instructing Initiative participants on Journaling, Mentoring and Breakthrough Plan development. He formally served as Executive Director of Urban Youth Leadership, a ministry to at-risk youth in urban Kansas City. With a degree in Mass Media Communications from Oral Roberts University and a Masters in Communications from Grand Valley State University, Gerald exercises his passion for writing by overseeing and contributing to the DeVos newsletter, website blogs, monthly eBlast and via a host of marketing and promotional materials. Gerald Bell is advisor to men's ministries at The Greater Allen AME Cathedral of New York. He and his family live in Fort Lee, NJ.

I was twenty-five years old before realizing my life was on a destructive course. It was not due to drug addiction, a criminal record or "baby daddy" drama. I simply lacked vision and a sense of purpose. I had all the energy and ambition of a typical mid-twenties urbanite seeking to escape the hood, yet clueless about how to direct it. Filled with passion for broadcast media and the music industry, I thought the only way to succeed was to get discovered. I was no different than today's inner- city youth who see sports or entertainment as their only option to make something of themselves. I was insecure and trusted no one. Therefore, I looked to no one but me, and as a result some of my best attributes were slowly being squandered. I later discovered that significance in life doesn't come to talented complacent people - it requires initiative.

That, along with a mentor, is what finally put me on a path toward fulfilling my dreams. An Elder at my church in Columbus, Ohio mentored me while I served with him in the church youth department. He knew I was raised by my mom in a single parent home. He knew how deeply my father's rejection and abandonment affected me. When a father never acknowledges his child, the impact is traumatizing. Getting older and moving on doesn't heal the affect. As the youngest of six siblings, he knew I grew up a spoiled brat. He also knew that I needed a firm "motivation" nudge to realize my untapped potential. Challenging me with tough questions, goal setting and holding me accountable - this high capacity leader with a family and countless responsibilities offered me one of life's most precious commodities - time.

Still struggling with trusting people, I was leery of him for a stint thinking that he wanted to abuse my talents to benefit the youth ministry. On a few occasions I tried to create situations for my mentor to betray me but it never worked. Our mentor mentee relationship included working on youth events, traveling to his preaching engagements, exercising at the gym and a host of activities that afforded us constructive time together. I ate dinner around the table with his family. I watched how he attentively listened to his wife's every word. I admired the respect his sons demonstrated for their father. I was privileged to hold his youngest daughter at birth. He was intentional about making sure I saw him in action.

But there were points along the way when I rebelled against his counsel. We'd argue about some of the decisions I was making, like packing up and moving to Los Angeles with no survival plans in place. I'd say, "I'm just trusting that God will make a way when I get there." He would always demonstrate patience and consistency. And like a prodigal son I later understood the wisdom he was imparting. Skilled at shifting hats, my mentor at times was more of a big brother. He'd counsel me about my broken relationships and poor choices. Other times he was like the dad I never had nurturing manhood, character and godliness in me. Often he'd wear the hat of a coach assigning me drills and plays that would strengthen my gift's sweet spot so when it was time for my "A" game I could deliver my best. Even some twenty years later he never fails to wear the hat of a trusted friend. I got to expose my darkest failures, insecurities and hurts, and my mentor's friendship remains unshaken.

There are many who would have concluded that it was too late for someone at my age to develop character, values and personal goals. Scientific data would likely have considered labeling me as set in my ways and it was too late to change. I may have been a late bloomer but I thank God for a Bible believing mentor who pounded in the writings of Paul, "And do not be conformed to this world but be transformed by renewing your mind..." Romans 12:2. I wish I had a quarter for every time I heard my mentor quote this passage of scripture.

Because of God's deliberate love and my mentor's belief in me, I buckled down and earned my Bachelor's and Master's degrees. I became gainfully employed in the field of philanthropy, and mustered up the faith to start a family. It's never too late to mentor someone willing to trust that God can do the impossible.

Gerald Bell, in his role as Communications Manager has written many newsletters and blogs for DeVos' Urban Leadership Initiative. Here are timely mentoring bullet points from one of his articles to youth pastors across the country:

- Mentor and mentee must share a compatible philosophy.
- The mentor should be knowledgeable in the subject and objective in his/her criticism.
- The mentor must genuinely believe in the potential of the mentee.
- A good mentor helps define the vision, the goal, and the plan.
- There must be good chemistry.
- The mentor helps develop options rather than decisions.
- The mentor must be able to commit to a person and to a situation.
- The mentor must be given permission to hold the mentee accountable.

The DeVos Urban Leadership Initiative is an intense 15-month tuition-sponsored leadership development program for urban youth workers. A person of influence in their local community nominates youth leaders to apply for this program. For more information about the DeVos Urban Leadership Initiative, please contact the Grand Rapids office at 616-643-4848 or send inquiries to the DeVos Urban Leadership Initiative, PO Box 230257, Grand Rapids, MI 49523-0257, or e-mail to staff@dvuli.org

Question to Ponder

1. It is hard for men to admit to their fears. What is a fear that you have overcome or you are still battling?

2. If God did not give us the spirit of fear where does fear come from?

3. Sometimes a fear can intrude because of another person or an act not in your control. Can you describe such a situation?

CHAPTER THIRTEEN

MENTORING CHILDREN OF INCARCERATED PARENTS

People were also bringing babies to Jesus to have Him touch them. When the disciples saw this, they rebuked them. But Jesus called the children to him and said, "Let the little children come to me, and do not hinder them, for the kingdom of God belongs to such as these. I tell you the truth, anyone who will not receive the kingdom of God like a little child will never enter it." Luke 18: 15-17

One of the soldiers on the battlefield addressing the needs of children of incarcerated parents is The Honorable Rev. Dr. Wilson B. Goode, former Mayor of Philadelphia, The City of Brotherly Love (And Sisterly Affection). He is now head of a national mentoring organization called Amachi which is an African word meaning, "Who knows but what God has brought us through this child." Amachi's tagline is: People of faith mentoring children of promise, a powerful reminder of the possibilities that are in all children.

This country locks up more people than any other nation in the world. There are more than 2.3 million people behind bars on parole or probation in America. That number, according to Pew Charitable Trust, means that more than 1 out of 100 Americans are in jail or prisons. It must be said that people who commit heinous crimes should be locked up, that is not the issue.

Yet the question begging for an answer is how will this nation prepare for over 633,000 people exiting the prison system yearly? The mass incarceration of people of color has wreaked havoc on families, communities and now threatens the prosperity of this nation. Nationwide, over 7,300,000 children have a parent (or parents) in jail, prison or under control of the penal system. It is probable, given the ever increasing number of people locked up, that children of prisoners are enrolled in mentoring programs.

It is important for mentors to know about the business of incarceration, recognizing how this system impacts the mentoring relationship, families and communities. In New York there are $1,000,000 Blocks. This is the cost of incarcerating people living on one street. Unfortunately there are far too many $1,000,000 blocks draining monies that could best be spent on schools, training programs, drug treatment and college scholarships. Unfortunately, the people that make policy decisions are comfortable with reactive deficit spending rather than proactive asset spending. Roughly translated this statement means: 'Why is it always easier to find lock em up dollars' but it is always difficult to identify 'hook em up dollars?'

Here are contextual facts that should help mentors appreciate the gravity of mentoring children of prisoners while also analyzing the growth of prisons in this country. Over the last two decades, American prisons moved from the concept of penitence (hence the term penitentiary) to correct antisocial behavior (Department of Correction) to the present day prison industrial complex (which some have called modern day slavery) where prison futures are traded on Wall Street.

The fact that prison has become big business should tell us that high recidivism rates are in the best interest of shareholders - in essence, making crime pay. This also makes an incarcerated father's presence scarce in the lives of their children. Given the dramatic rise of women in the penal system, some children may have both parents locked up. These children either live in what is called kinship foster care with relatives (usually grandmothers) or go into the foster care system.

The big buildup in prison population happened after stringent drug laws were passed in state after state as part of The War on Drugs. The large number of nonviolent drug users arrested (and denied drug treatment as an option) disproportionately and unfairly fell on people of color. In New York State, The Rockefeller Drug Laws were passed mandating that a person convicted of possessing a certain weight of a controlled substance could get a mandatory sentence of 15 years to life even if this was a first offense. Women who stayed with men that were in the drug trade also were arrested in large number and subject to the same harsh penalties. The result of these egregious sentences stripped families of fathers and mothers and overburdened grandparents to provide childcare. Children deprived of their parents increasingly took to the streets and looked to gangs to offer what was missing in their lives, namely, a sense of family.

When a father comes home from prison it will take time for him to adjust. It should be said that the mentoring relationship should also adjust accordingly. One of the best things a mentoring program can do is help a returning father find needed services. There are reentry programs in some states to find employment, identify training opportunities, provide housing assistance, legal help as well as individual, family and marital counseling. Houses of worship, seminaries and civic groups could also host forums where returning citizens can present individual and family needs and challenges. While it is good to have prison ministry teams visiting and praying for the incarcerated, it is equally important to have options once the person returns to the community, especially if they knock on the church's door for help.

Questions to Ponder

1. What services can your church/mentoring program offer to parents of mentees that may be returning home from a correction facility?

2. What message do you think is centermost to consistently stress to a child with an incarcerated parent?

3. Imagine if you were locked up and had to write a letter to your son whom have not seen since birth. What would you say?

MENTOR'S SPIRITUAL REFLECTION
GOD'S UPSIDE DOWN CREW (GUDC)
Acts 17:5-6 (NKJV)

The scripture read in your hearing is a New Testament account of damage done to the Enemy's turf by brave, bold, bodacious members of God's Upside Down Crew. You never heard of God's Upside Down Crew (GUDC)? Well, let me tell you who they are. This team for righteousness believed that Jesus was the Son of God and was crucified, died and was buried and on the third day arose with all power in his hands. The leader GUDC was a man named Paul. But before he would lead GUDC he ran with the Evil Wrecking Crew (EWC). EWC persecuted Christians as they kept a stranglehold on tradition that choked people to death on the streets.

Paul angered people because he questioned and rejected established religious beliefs. Paul and his crew led people away from idol worship and put phony prophets out of business. He angered people throughout Rome, Jerusalem Asia Minor and beyond and did hard time because he spoke truth to power. His critics, and there were many, claimed that Paul and his followers were guilty of turning the world upside down. I wonder if I can recruit you into GUDC. It does not matter if you have been running with The Evil Wrecking Crew as late as last night. Now be clear: don't expect to see a long line of your peers eager to join GUDC. Some of your friends won't join GUDC because it will mean giving up some things that seem too important.

But for those who want to be on the Lord's side I must say this to you in all honesty: Before You Can Turn The World Upside Down - You Must Fight To Turn Your Life God Side Up. Allow me to drop some God Side Up Wisdom on young and not so young alike:

1. **You Must Want To Be Turned God Side Up**—Without perspiration there can never be sustained transformation. You have to want God more than you want the world.

2. **You Must Be Willing To Make Sacrifices For Your Wants**—All people have wants but not everyone is willing to pay the cost. Dreams cost and you have to do some upfront investment to get some backend dividends.

3. **You Must Invest In Yourself And Don't Be Cheap**—Some brothers have totally misappropriated their life investment responsibility by always helping others and ignoring their own dry funds. Life is like a bank, no deposits no withdrawals.

4. **You Must Watch Who You Run Behind**—Everybody moving with you is not necessarily traveling with you. You need to cut some folk

loose. That is your responsibility not your parents, teachers, youth minister or the pastor.

5. **You Must Not Impair Your On-Board Computer**—God has given his creation the greatest super computer in the world (the mind) to regulate the most complicated machine ever constructed. Take care of your mind and your mind will take care of you.

6. **You Must Reject Mediocrity and Strive For Personal, Academic and Spiritual Excellence**—Unfortunately there are too many people happy to be either an invisible nobody or settle on being ½ of somebody. Greatness is in you but it is your job to find it.

7. **You Must Always Watch Your Step**—One step can take you closer to your dream or closer to your nightmare. One step can mean life or death, freedom or incarceration. Just one false step can mean parenthood, STD's or HIV/AIDS or death. Please watch your step.

Now that you have the Seven Musts for turning your life God Side Up you must do one more thing: Believe in your heart and confess with your mouth that Jesus Christ is Lord and beloved the power to turn the world upside down will fall on you. Now you are officially down with GUDC!

MENTOR'S TESTIMONY
THE CHALLENGE AND OPPORTUNITY OF
MENTORING
Rev. Maurice D. Winley

Maurice Winley is Chaplain for St. Christopher Inc., an adolescent residential facility in Westchester County. He has extensive experience as a consultant for adolescent correctional facilities around the country. He is a sought after youth development trainer and lecturer passionately speaking on issues that impact at-risk youth. Rev Winley is Youth Pastor of Soul Saving Station Church in Harlem. He is married and is the father of a young son.

I am a third generation mentor. As a son of a pastor whose father was also a pastor, I have inherited the passion for mentorship. I focus my ministry on urban youth development, community organization and education. As a Black male Christian, and now as a father, I believe my calling is to help the generation of vulnerable young people of color that we are losing to drugs and street violence, especially young Black males.

Over the past 16 years, I have been engaged with the full spectrum of vulnerable youth in numerous systems and settings, including youth involved in the criminal justice systems in New York City, Westchester County and Long Island. I have aided troubled adolescents in residential treatment facilities, special education schools districts and public schools. I have shared some dark days especially pain with these young people. They are hurting and need healing.

My life experience is not so different from that of the young people with whom I work. I grew up in New York in the inner-city; I have had my own share of pain. As a result I am sensitive to their life circumstances and I am able to engender their trust. I speak to youth in ways that challenge them to think about their lives, examine their core values and to change their convictions. I engage young people in activities that afford them opportunities for positive character development. I empower them to take responsibility for themselves and to become involved in community by showing compassion and care for others. I tell them, "Accept guidance; keep your hearts and minds open to the Spirit of God. The choices you make are the choices you are going to live by. Don't become a prisoner of your own bitterness. Don't act out of pain. Don't become what has hurt you." More often than not they receive that message.

I believe men of color have a unique opportunity to profoundly impact this generation of young Black men through mentoring. The so called professionals can't do it alone. It takes every caring, responsible male in our community to accept their role as mentors. Every man has value that he can share with a young person; our lives are a curriculum, if we are brave enough to become an open book.

However, somewhere in our own quest for significance as African American men we have inadvertently created a pandemic of fatherlessness, failing to take hold of our greatest purpose which is to train our sons to be men. This failure has polarized youth who are left vulnerable, unable to authentically connect with other men, wallowing in the devastation of insignificance. We have an opportunity to break this cycle. If we are honest we can admit that an absentee father knows he has failed. This is one of the deepest wounds a man can experience.

We retreat or withdraw when we sense our own failure and shame, and mentoring is neglected. It is easy to talk about our successes, but much more difficult to talk about our problems. We hide our disappointments and failures, scars which inhibit truthful communication. Yet, behind those scars are fountains of wisdom. When this reality is accessed through genuine introspection, then revelation for true transformation can be received. The redemptive value is exponential for those who disclose their own weakness and failures and for that, a young mentee avoids the cycle of insignificance.

Our young men need mentors who are spiritually mature and who can shed their masks. They need men who are able to be honest and transparent, to engage in open, true dialogue. Mentors need to be able to say, "These are the mistakes I have made, I messed up here, don't do it." The Scriptures declare, "Confess your faults one to another, and pray for one another that you may be healed. The effectual, fervent prayer of a righteous man availeth much." James 5:18.

Transparency is cleansing and healing for both mentor and mentee. The greater joy for the child of God comes in seeing a young man give his life to Christ. Young people respond to heartfelt connectedness. My work is to build rock solid, lifelong relationships. I want to see the young men I mentor become positive role models for the next generation. I want to be blessed to officiate at their weddings and to dedicate their children to God, rather than mourning with their mothers at their funerals. If we can save one young man we can begin to save an entire generation. Mentoring is the first big step in that awesome, wonderfully privileged process.

MENTOR MISSION FUEL
BILL OF RIGHTS FOR CHILDREN OF INCARCERATED PARENTS

As mentioned, I am a Board member of The Osborne Association located in New York. Osborne is a member of the San Francisco Children of Incarcerated Parents Partnership. The Bill of Rights is taken from their website.

1. **I have the right to be safe and informed at the time of my parent's arrest.**

Many children are introduced to the criminal justice system when their parent is arrested and they see her taken away in handcuffs. Most police departments do not have protocols for addressing the needs of children when a parent is arrested. The resulting experience can be terrifying and confusing for the children left behind. Some wind up in the back of a police car themselves, on the way to the first in a series of temporary placements. Others are left behind in, or return home to, empty apartments. Arrested parents often prefer not to involve public agencies in the lives of their children, out of fear of losing custody. Many children share this fear, but at the same time long for someone to notice and attend to the family's vulnerabilities that can both lead to and result from a parent's arrest.

> **Factoid:** *70 percent of children who were present at a parent's arrest watched that parent being handcuffed and 30 percent were confronted with drawn weapons.*

2. **I have the right to be heard when decisions are made about me.**

When a parent is arrested children whose lives may already have left them with little sense of control often feel even more alienated from the events that swirl around them. Adults they have never met remove their parents with little explanation, then decide where children will go without consulting them. When children continue to feel unheard within the institutions that govern their lives in their parents' absence, their sense of powerlessness grows.

> **Factoid:** *Three in 100 American children will go to sleep tonight with a parent in jail or prison and one in eight African-American children have a parent behind bars.*

3.   I have the right to be considered when decisions are made about my parent.

Increasingly tough sentencing laws, which have caused the U.S. prison population to increase fivefold over the past three decades, have also had a tremendous impact on children. But as it stands, sentencing law not only does not require judges to consider children when they make decisions that will affect their lives profoundly; in some cases, it actively forbids them from doing so. A more sensible and humane policy would take into account the fact that sentencing decisions will inevitably affect family members—especially children—and strive to protect their interests as much as possible without compromising public safety.

> **Factoid:** *Nearly three quarters of those admitted to state prison have been convicted of no violent crimes.*

4.   I have the right to be well cared for in my parent's absence.

When a child loses a parent to incarceration, he also loses a home. In the most extreme cases, children may wind up fending for themselves in a parent's absence. Some will spend time in the foster care system, where 97 percent of administrators say they have no specific policy in place to address those children's needs. The majority stay with relatives, often elderly and impoverished grandmothers who may be strained personally and financially by the challenge of caring for a second generation.

Factoid: *Half of all children with incarcerated mothers are cared for by grandparents.*

5. I have the right to speak with, see and touch my parent.

Visiting an incarcerated parent can be difficult and confusing for children, but research suggests that contact between prisoners and their children benefits both, reducing the chance of parents returning to prison and improving the emotional life of children. Because increasing numbers of incarcerated parents are held at prohibitive distances from their children, too many children are denied the opportunity for contact with their parents. In 1978, only eight percent of women prisoners had ever received a visit from their children. By 1999, 54 percent had not received a single visit.

> **Factoid:** *Prisoners who have regular visits are six times less likely to reenter prison than those who have none.*

6. I have the right to receive support as I face my parent's incarceration.

Children whose parents are imprisoned carry tremendous burdens. Not only do they lose the company and care of a parent, they also must deal with the stigma of parental incarceration, and fear for their parent's safety and well-being. Researchers who have interviewed children who have experienced parental incarceration have found them vulnerable to depression, anger and shame. One study found many showed symptoms of post-traumatic stress reaction—difficulty sleeping and concentrating, depression, and flashbacks to their parents' crimes or arrests. In the face of these difficulties, many young people will tell you that they rarely receive the support they need as they "do time" along with their parents.

> **Factoid:** *Only six state child welfare systems have a policy in place to address the needs of children of incarcerated parents.*

7. I have the right not to be judged, blamed or labeled because my parent is incarcerated.

Incarceration carries with it a tremendous stigma. Because young children identify with their parents, they are likely to internalize this stigma, associating themselves with the labels placed on their parents or blaming themselves for their parents' absence. As they grow older, many report feeling blamed or stigmatized by others—neighbors, peers, teachers and other authority figures, even family members—because of their parents' situation. Some try to keep a parent's incarceration secret. Many describe the shame and stigma they have experienced as the heaviest burden they carry, lasting long after a parent is released or a child grows up.

> **Factoid:** *1 in 10 children of prisoners will be incarcerated before reaching the age of 18.*

8. I have the right to a lifelong relationship with my parent

Abiding family bonds are the strongest predictor there is of successful prisoner reentry. For children, sustained attachments form the building blocks for successful development. But changes in child welfare law, specifically, accelerated timetables for termination of parental rights—have increased the odds that even a relatively short sentence will lead to the permanent severance of family bonds. When this happens, children are forced to forfeit the most fundamental right of all - the right to remain part of their families.

Factoid: *Appellate cases involving termination of prisoner's parental rights have gone up 250% since 1997.*

For more information, resources and publications on children of incarcerated go to www.sfcipp.org

Question to Ponder

1. What do you think was the most staggering factoid presented in The Bill of Rights?

2. What could your congregation do to address policy concerns about the rights of children of incarcerated parents in your state?

3. As far as you know, are you mentoring a child with an incarcerated parent? If so what steps do you think important to take?

MENTOR'S TESTIMONY
KNOCK KNOCK...WHO'S THERE...? WE ARE
By Daniel Beaty

Daniel Beaty is an award-winning actor, singer, writer, and composer. Last season he had an extended off-Broadway run of his acclaimed solo play THROUGH THE NIGHT produced by Daryl Roth. For this production Daniel received 2011 Lucille Lortel, Drama Desk, Drama League and Outer Critics Circle nominations. Daniel also received the 2010 AUDELCO

Award for Outstanding Solo Performance and the 2010 Ovation Award for Best Male Lead Actor. His critically acclaimed solo play Emergence-See! ran off-Broadway to a sold-out, extended run at The Public Theater in the fall of 2006. For this production, he received the 2007 Obie Award for Excellence in Off-Broadway Theater for Writing & Performing and the 2007 AUDELCO Award for Solo Performance. He is the recipient of the 2007 Scotsman Fringe First Award for the best new writer at the Edinburgh Festival and was presented with a Lamplighter Award from the Black Leadership Forum in Washington D.C. In the spring of 2008, Emergence-See!, now re-titled Emergency had a sold-out seven-week engagement at the Geffen Playhouse in Los Angeles and was awarded two 2009 NAACP Theater Awards including Best Actor. Daniel has worked throughout the U.S., Europe, and Africa performing on programs with artists such as Ruby Dee, Ossie Davis, Jill Scott, Sonia Sanchez, MC Lyte, Mos Def, Tracy Chapman, Deepak Chopra, and Phylicia Rashad. He holds a BA with Honors in English & Music from Yale University and an MFA in Acting from the American Conservatory Theatre. He also has a new solo play on the life of Paul Robeson – The Tallest Tree in the Forest. He is a proud member of New Dramatists and an Adjunct Professor at Columbia University. Both Emergency & Through the Night are available online. His first children's book based on his poem Knock Knock is slated to be released by Little Brown Books in 2013.

As a boy I shared a game with my father.
We played it every morning 'till I was three.

He would knock knock on my door
And I'd pretend to be asleep 'till he got right next to the bed
Then I would get up and jump into his arms.
Good morning papa.
And my Papa, he would tell me that he loved me.
We shared a game...knock knock.
'Till the day the knock never came
And my mama takes me on a ride
Past cornfields, on this never-ending highway,
'Till we reach a place of high rusty gates
A confused little boy, I enter the building
Carried in my mama's arms...knock knock
We reach a room of windows and brown faces.
Behind one of the windows sits my father.
I jump out of my mama's arms and run joyously towards my papa's
Only to be confronted by this window
I knock knock trying to break through the glass, trying to get to my father
I knock knock as my mama pulls me away before my papa even says a word.
And for years he has never said a word….

December 1995. It is Christmas break during my sophomore year at Yale. I'm back home in Dayton, Ohio and I've decided to do it. I'm going to visit my father in prison. This will be the first time I have seen my father in more years than I can remember—at least ten. As I ride in the car next to my mother, all manner of thoughts and emotions course through me. Do I look him? What if he doesn't like me? What if I don't like him?

I arrive at the prison, a massive gray and brown industrial complex. A large, muscular, imposing guard stands at the counter as I enter the first door.

Take everything out of your pockets and place it that basket.

I do as I am instructed, terrified. As I remove my keys from my pocket, my wallet, I can feel the sweatiness of my palms. The guard presses a buzzer. Buzz. A gate opens.

Enter through here.

Gate one. Slam. Buzz. Another gate opens. Gate two. Slam.

I enter a room of tables and brown faces. Fathers with their children, girlfriends, mothers, wives sit not touching but with a longing to touch pouring from their eyes. Some of the men are chained around their ankles, some also around their wrists—but most have hands that are free at least.

Anxiously, I stare in the direction from which I see the men arriving and departing. I feel my chest beating in my throat and I swallow hard, eager and afraid to see my father. He enters wearing a bright orange jump suit, salt and pepper hair. He's much older than I remember. The guard removes the chains around his ankles, around his wrists. Thank God. He walks slowly towards me and opens his arms. And I jump. Knock Knock.

In this moment, I am once again the little boy that longed for his daddy. In this moment, all the love I felt for him as a small child comes flooding back to me. As I sit and listen to his stories—some certainly lies and excuses, I devour every word desperate for them to be true—desperate to understand, to believe that his choices, his abandonment were not my fault.

The layers and complexities of my emotions would come later—rage, sadness, grief for time lost, accountability, truth. But in this initial visit, the dominant feeling is love.

And for years he has never said a word....
And so I write these words for the little boy in me
Who still awaits his papa's knock:
Papa come home 'cause I miss you,
Miss you waking me in the mornings and telling me you love me.
Papa come home 'cause there's things I don't know
And I thought maybe you could teach me
How to shave, how to dribble a ball,
How to talk to a lady, walk like a man,
Papa come home 'cause I decided a while back
I want to be just like you but I've forgotten who you are.
And fifteen years later a little boy cries and so I speak these words and try to heal,
Try to father myself and I dream up
A father who says the words my father did not--
Dear Son, I'm sorry I never came home.
For every lesson I failed to teach, hear these words:
Shave in one direction with strong deliberate strokes to avoid irritation.
Dribble the page with the brilliance of your ballpoint pen.
Walk like a god and your goddess will come to you.
No longer will I be there to knock on your door so you must learn to knock for yourself.

Throughout the course of my life my father has been arrested 58 times. The arrest that impacted my life the most is the one I describe in my poem "Knock Knock." As a three year-old boy, my mother took me to visit my father in prison and he was behind a glass – I could not reach him. And he remained unreachable for the most of my growing up – with the exception of the brief moments when he would reappear before being arrested again. As a three year-old child, my primary caregiver, my father abandoned me and the safety of his physical and emotional presence was no longer available to me. The world as I had always known it was thrown out of order.

Children need to feel safe. They need to be held, told they are loved, and have the consistency of loving parents and community support. Unfortunately, too many of our children are not afforded such a nurturing, embracing environment. With my father's abandonment due to his incarceration, I had a subtle yet pervasive thought that I was destined to follow in my father's footsteps. Even as I accepted one of the highest honors upon graduating from Yale University, I had a private feeling that I was an imposter, and would eventually be found out. My father was in prison and had been there all my life. Who was I to think my path could be so different?

Knock knock down doors of racism and poverty I could not.

Knock knock on doors of opportunity for the lost brilliance of the black men who crowd these cells.

Knock knock with diligence for the sake of your children.

Knock knock for me for as long as you are free these prison gates cannot contain my spirit; the best of me still lives in you.

Knock knock with the knowledge that you are my son, but you are not my choices.
Yes, we are our father's sons and daughters, but we are not their choices
For despite their absences we are still here.
Still alive...
Still breathing...
With the power to change this world one little boy and girl at a time—

Mentorship is the healing salve that is so desperately needed. The greatest way to control the possibility of a people is to control their images of themselves. All children including black boys need to see images of themselves as possible and free. All children including black boys need three-dimensional, living, breathing, consistently present examples of the greatness they can become.

Knock knock...
Who's there?
We are.

CHAPTER FOURTEEN

MENTOR'S PROVERBIAL WISDOM

My son, if you accept my words and store up my commands within you, turning your ear to wisdom and applying your heart to understanding and if you call out for insight and cry aloud for understanding and if you look for it as for silver and search for it as a hidden treasure then you will understand the fear of the Lord and find the knowledge of God. Proverbs 2:1-6

The Book of Proverbs joins Psalms, Ecclesiastes, Song of Solomon and Job to form the genre called wisdom literature. A good mentor must have wisdom and be willing to pass it along to his mentee. Proverbs is full of timeless spiritual and practical truisms that are helpful in mentoring, ministry and life. When the mentor and mentee are both jointly engaged in pursuing knowledge, wisdom and understanding, a strong bond is created. It is out of this bond that behavior and expectations can be elevated, goals met and lives transformed. With that said, look at these scriptures and harvest meaning for mentoring, life and spiritual growth.

- *A fool finds pleasure in evil conduct, but a man of understanding delights in wisdom. Proverbs 10:23*

- *Whoever loves discipline loves knowledge, but he who hates correction is stupid. Proverbs 12:1*

- *Reckless words pierce like a sword, but the tongue of the wise brings healing. Proverbs 12:18*

- *The prudent man keeps his knowledge in himself but the heart of fools blurts out folly. Proverbs 13:23*

- *A simple man believes anything but a prudent man gives thoughts to his steps. Proverbs 14:15*

- *A truthful witness saves lives but a false witness is deceitful. Proverbs 14: 25*

- *A heart of peace gives life to the body, but envy rots the bones. Proverbs 14:30*

- *A gentle answer turns away wrath but a harsh word stirs up anger. Proverbs 15:1*

- *Pride goes before destruction a haughty spirit before a fall. Proverbs 16:1*

- *All a man's ways seem innocent to him but motives are weighed by the Lord. Proverbs 16:2*

- *Commit to the Lord whatever you do and your plans will succeed. Proverbs 16:3*

- *A fool finds no pleasure in understanding but delights in airing his own opinions. Proverbs 18:2*

- *Many are the plans of a man's heart but it is the Lord's purpose that prevails. Proverbs 19:21*

- *Better is an open rebuke than hidden love. Proverbs 27:5*

Questions to Ponder

1. Which Proverb still challenges you the most? Why is that so?

2. What Proverb do you vividly recall using that changed you and/or a situation involving you?

3. Can you identify ways that you can use these or other sayings in an interactive way to open wisdom's door of dialogue between you and your mentee?

MENTOR'S SPIRITUAL REFLECTION
IN GOD WE TRUST
Proverbs 3:1-10

The scripture lesson admonishes God's people to place their trust in the Lord. It may seem ironic to talk to the very elect, to the ecclesia, about trusting God. Before you think this word is for someone else, or wonder why this word about trusting God is geared to saved, sanctified, Holy Ghost filled and fire baptized men, I ask that you hang with me for a while. Proverbs is an instructive aid for those who seek wisdom. Job and Ecclesiastes are more philosophical, tackling the thorny subjects of why the good have to suffer (theodicy), or why evil doers prosper.

Proverbs claims as its chief scribe, King Solomon, reputed to be one of the wisest men ever born. It is thought that Solomon borrowed some of his wise sayings from other sages from Egypt, Babylon, Mesopotamia and Palestine. The best way to understand Proverbs is to approach it from the perspective of what good parents would say to their child in an effort to help him live a more rewarding life. The Hebraic definition of Proverbs means to "taunt" or "parable". A more modern definition would include wise sayings. The type of literature found in Proverbs, ranges from: poetry, comparisons and contrasts, admonishments and two-line if/then couplets. Proverbs is rich in metaphors that help the reader see mental images of what is being taught.

Likewise, Proverbs was intended to teach people how to distinguish between the way of the wise and the way of fools. How many of you know that just because you grow up does not always mean that you mature? The Hebrew scholars were serious about discourse that differentiated the way of wisdom from the way of the fool. So much so, the Hebraic scholars ascribed five different categories of fools:

- Peti (open) naive, untutored, a simpleton, a natural born fool
- Kesil (dull, obtuse) insensitive to wisdom, and disinterested
- Ewil (stubborn) head-strong, willful, not teachable
- Litz (full of scorn) sits above God's wisdom, mocks those who take it seriously
- Nabal (proud fool) is a composite of all the fools and the worse of the lot—this person follows his or her own rules and acts as if there is no God.

The process of building and then walking in trust is not as easy as one would think. I looked up the word trust and after coming across several entries this one caught my eye: trust - to expect with assurance. I expand this definition saying: to expect that where and whom you place your hopes, your dreams, your vulnerability, your family, your fears, your future is big enough, is powerful enough, is faithful enough to come through. What you ultimately believe in is what you worship and what you worship becomes your "god" with a small 'g '. Let's look at some small 'g ' gods that circumvent our trusting in God with our whole heart, mind, spirit and finances. Perhaps you believe when the chips are down that:

1. **Family and friends will help you out.** They can do only but so much. In fact if you catch them between paydays, they may forget that they said if you run short, I got your back.

2. **Your job is your security blanket.** You are always there, working on the weekends. Your family rarely sees you. You can't go to church because there are dollars in the street to be made – until you get a pink slip .

3. **Trust rooted in the stock market.** You firmly believe that your portfolio is going to save you, your pension or money under the mattress will be there in time of need. Markets have cycles, pension funds raided and one catastrophic sickness can wipe out savings.

4. **Over Reliance On Temporal Things.** Your trust is in your natural ability, your charm, physicality, or education. All these attributes will eventually fade, grow dull, sag, or just not

matter as much over time. Alzheimer's or any other debilitating disease can rob you of your personality and book knowledge.

If you placed your trust in something or someone else that is clearly a disappointing small "g" god it is not too late to wise up and put your trust in God. As long as you have breath in your body and a real desire for wisdom it can be attained. Don't allow yourself to become mired in the mud of foolishness. Don't be like Nabal (1Samuel 25), the sum of all of fools. The fear of the Lord, the knowledge of God is the beginning of wisdom. Here are some "TRUST BUILDERS" from Proverbs:

1. *Proverbs 3:5-10 Trust in the Lord with all of your heart, and lean not to your own understanding; and in all your ways acknowledge Him and He will direct your path. Do not be wise in your own eyes, fear the Lord and shun evil. This will bring health to your body and nourishment to your bones.*

2. *Proverbs 28:25 A greedy man stirs up dissension, but he who trusts in the Lord will prosper.*

3. *Proverbs 29:25 Fear of man will prove to be a snare, but whoever trusts in the Lord is kept safe.*

Now we are going to have a quiz on what to do when trust-busting occurrences intrude on life. I will give you the right answer in advance so there is no way you can fail. All you have to do after each statement is say out loud: In God We Trust.

- When my enemies conspire and come against me
- When the doctor says there's nothing more I can do
- When I am lied on by a friend, co-worker or loved one
- When depression tries to pull me down in a dark pit
- When the bill collectors won't leave me alone
- When I stand between God's promise and His answer
- When I feel all alone and my tears soak my pillow
- When I don't have two quarters to rub together.
- When bad memories or non-forgiveness overtake me
- When past failure tries to sabotage my future promise

My brothers I was once in deep tribulation in my 20's when I found the Lord for real. My assigned inner-terrorists of fear, doubt and self-loathing tried to take me out. I was a fool. I was a big, sad, an educated Nabal, lost in the land of Nabals. But it was in this sorry state that I found God. I prayed for help. I prayed for deliverance. I had no other choice. I had to trust in God. It did not matter that I went to Howard University or Columbia's Teacher's College. My parents loved me, but they could not save me. I had to go to the rock that was higher than I. That's my story now what's yours?

I remember when I was a child and attended a small store-front church in Harlem. Every time the offering was taken the congregation would recite this passage of scripture that I learned from childhood:

Some trust in chariots and some in horses; but we will remember the name of the Lord our God. They have bowed down and fallen; but we have risen up and stand upright. Save, Lord! May the King answer us when we call. Psalm 20:7-9 NKJV

I didn't know what all that meant then but today I choose to trust in God. Do you really trust in God? Is He your anchor, your sustainer, your heavy load sharer? Don't be foolish. Trust in God for all of your needs.

MENTOR'S MISSION FUEL
PRACTICAL WISDOM SAYINGS

When I was a child my mother would send me to the store to buy a head of cabbage and I would bring home a head of lettuce. When she would send me for a head of lettuce-well you probably guessed what happened. I could not figure out why two things that were so much alike where kept so close together. In my mind I thought cabbage and lettuce should be on opposite sides of the store. Since I am confessing, I also have to admit that I got tomato sauce and tomato paste mixed up too.

After this happened more than a few times I remember my mother saying something to me that in retrospect changed my life. She said, "Boy you are smart but you don't have common sense." It was at that precise moment that I decided that I had to get common sense even though I did not know what it was, how to get it, where to get it-or how to keep it.

The desire to have common sense has served me well. I have worked with more talented, smarter or creative people but in many instances, I came out ahead because they lacked common sense. I have to confess that I made some decisions while growing up that were devoid of any inkling of common sense. It was only the hand of God that shielded me from the consequences of my foolishness.

Lacking common sense at any age can be deadly. While it may seem funny when a child can't differentiate between lettuce from cabbage, it is no laughing matter when a teen knows a car is stolen and rides in it anyway; or when a grown man agrees to hide a 'hot' gun in his house for a dicey friend only to have his youngest child take it to elementary school to show friends. Common sense is really not that common.

Please accept my folksy homage to common sense in the form of sayings that are laden with life wisdom for all to look at but only a few will see. I have heard many of these axioms over the course of my life. They are not intended to be exhaustive-just serve as a point of wisdom departure:

- God bless the child who has his own.
- Don't worry about tomorrow, tomorrow will take care of itself.
- He who laughs last laughs best.
- Can't help others if you can't help yourself.
- If you are the smartest in your group find a new group.
- Little people talk about people big people talk about ideas.
- Do unto others as you would have them do unto you.
- If you don't live life, who will live it for you?
- Every tub must rest on its own bottom.

- Your true value is the one you place on yourself.
- Don't cry over spilt milk.
- Lift as you climb.
- When spiders unite they can tie up the lion.
- Don't put off until tomorrow what can be done today.
- The squeaky wheel gets the most oil.
- Keep your mouth shut and your ears open.
- Doing nothing when doing something is required is the worst thing you can do.
- No man is an island no man stands alone.
- If there's no enemy inside then the enemy outside can never harm you.
- Better alone than in bad company.
- Lay down with dogs get up with fleas.
- The first 100 years are the hardest.
- Your troubles will show you the road.
- The hardest rain will not wash off the leopard's spots.
- You make your bed hard you have to sleep in it.
- Do what is right not what is popular.
- If you don't know where you are going any direction will do.
- Bloom where you are planted.
- Take nothing personal respond constructively rather than defensively.

- Look in before looking out.
- Come home clean or stay away dirty.
- Don't make wrong right or right wrong.
- You have to play the hand dealt to you.
- Don't hate people who love you and love people that hate you.
- Into each life some rain must fall.

Questions To Ponder

1. If you were ask to do a 5 minute reflection on a saying that spoke to your spirit which one would you choose (then write it out)?

2. Can you identify three sayings you are familiar with that were not selected yet you feel are important to include?

3. Can you find a way to incorporate these and other wisdom sayings into teachable lessons for your mentee? If so how would you do it?

MENTOR'S TESTIMONY
I GOT YOUR BACK (BUT YOU HAVE TO STAND ON YOUR OWN TWO FEET)
By Eugene Adams

Eugene (Gene) Adams serves as Bronx Community College's Director of Collaborative Programs, in which he oversees partnerships with over 25 schools and serves over 2,000 students annually. He also advises the BCC African Students Association and the Amadou Diallo Foundation Inc. Adams has also founded Kid Comic Con, an annual family-based graphic art and literacy event which is intended to encourage the artistic and literary talents of more children and adolescents of color. KCC brings out seasoned artist, writers, editors, and others who volunteer their time and love of comic book and art to the Bronx community. Adams states, "Our children have tremendous artistic talent and creative imagination. We must support both their artistic interest and passion. Far too often we as parents, educators, and program directors don't fully support our children's art interests by putting them in programs, advocating for more arts funding, or simply turning off the television and engaging them is drawing, dance, music, or other artistic activities". Bro. Gene Adams is an accomplished long time commercial and documentary photographer and he has curated a new photography exhibition, "African Transitions", which chronicles the African continent over the past three decades. Bro Gene Adams, going back to the 80's, has taken countless young people to Africa and has adopted the Senegalese-American Bilingual School (SABS), a small Pre-K through twelfth grade school in Dakar that serves 700 students. Bro Adams also brought the Cheikh Anta Diop, Senegal's most well-known university, to the BCC campus. Bro. Eugene Adams enjoys Senegalese hip-hop in the rare moments of spare time. He counts his own grandparents as his own personal superheroes.

My name is Gene Adams. I was born in a small community on Long Island. My family migrated to New York from South Carolina and Georgia during the "Great Black Migration" of the early 20th Century. Like many of the black families that came north looking for better opportunities, my family lacked education and skills and as a result had to work in low paying jobs as maids and janitors. Luckily, I was raised by my grandparents, though uneducated, [they] were hardworking and exceptionally intelligent. They encouraged me and instilled strong values. They also would not allow me to give up on myself or dreams.

As a child, I was very sickly and physically weak. I stuttered when I spoke and had elephant size ears. To make things worse I suffered from a condition known as dyslexia. Dyslexia is a learning condition that impacts on your ability to read, write and have good physical coordination. Other kids laughed at me a lot because, I read poorly, had terrible handwriting, and was horrible at sports. I was always the last one chosen when we played dodgeball, basketball, or any other activity that called for good coordination. On top of all of these problems, the school I went to placed me in a "special class" in the fifth grade. I was depressed, picked on and an outsider.

Throughout all this though, I had my grandparents always there telling me how bright and important I was. In spite of all of my obvious challenges I was taught to see myself as valuable. The most important gift they gave me was the ability to define myself in my own terms. I struggled through school but never gave up. I found out what my strengths were and concentrated on them. I graduated from high school with mediocre grades.

The college I attended had remedial classes and I enrolled in workshops to improve my reading, writing and math skills. I developed my visual and artistic talents and became a professional photographer. My experience with my grandparents helped me become a good listener. I also became a counselor. While I was poor in team sports, I excelled in martial arts because I could do it at my own pace and earned a black belt.

My grandparents taught me to value not only myself but also other people and the gift of life. As a child I was angry and wanted to simply give up. I later learned that life is always changing and we are always presented with new opportunities to make things different. There are many people like my grandparents who are willing to encourage and help us. We have to always be looking out for them and willing to accept the help when it is offered. As my grandparents would always say, "I got your back but you have to stand up on your own two feet."

CHAPTER FIFTEEN

MENTOR'S RESCUE PARADOX

A longing fulfilled is sweet to the soul, but fools detest turning from evil. Proverbs 13:19

The premise of romantic fairy tales contains the thought about Prince Charming, riding on a white steed, galloping to the rescue of a damsel in distress. There are movies, books and television programs that have made a fortune off of this simple theme. The writers of romance novels as well as fairy tales know that a rescuer has awesome mythical power in the eyes and heart of the person in need of assistance. There is nothing more alluring and desired than a rescuer. The rescuer is a hero. The rescuer comes to make wrong right. The rescuer, always a man, sweeps the woman off her feet and they all live happy ever after. Now that is a great fairy tale.

When this rescuer theme is played out in the mentor/mentee family relationship it can have disastrous consequences. Men, it is incumbent upon you to not fall into the mentor rescue paradox. A paradox is an inconsistency or self-contradiction where you start out with the goal of doing one thing and an opposite conclusion pops up. To be clear, if a mentor is perceived as the prayed for rescuer of a woman's child, he can take on aspects of the proverbial knight in shining armor on a mission to save the damsel in distress. It is not only the woman that can have this feeling; the man may feel that he IS the rescuer that will save the young lad from self-destruction (no dragons in this tale).

So now we have the mentor and the mom of the mentee engaged in a fairy tale reality and the script is set.

The attraction could also be real but it will never be right. This feeling, if not recognized and checked, can open a door to an illicit sexual relationship that has nothing to do with mentoring and everything to do with taking advantage of a situation. While a mentor is called to help - he can't help himself to what does not belong to him.

A man called to mentor, whether married or single, must not misuse the trust given to him. Having a mentoring relationship with the child and a sexual relationship with the child's mother is destructive to the child, church, mentoring program and is a sin. What I know about human nature (the flesh) is that it can never be satisfied. I also know what is done in secret will be exposed in public because people talk (young people talk).

Now it does take two to tango and the woman in this "fairy tale dance" must also exercise high judgment and discipline. A mentor helping your son is not a convenient substitute boyfriend. He is not your husband nor is he the boy's father. A mentor is a man trying to help your child - he is not your Prince Charming. No scriptures about Boaz or Bathsheba will justify having a sleazy affair because everybody involved will be hurt. It is imperative to drive home this point because we live in a time when the prevailing thought is if it feels good to you then it has to be good for you.

This is not just the pervasive philosophy of the world. Tragically, this same destructive energy has crept into the church. It lodges in the flesh of frustrated men and women, or conscienceless opportunists who are double-agents, scouring the pews and pulpits, picking off the vulnerable, confused and needy. It is hard to say no with your mouth if there is a yes in your flesh. This reality does not make for a good fairy tale but it surely is a needed ingredient for a tragedy.

Perhaps it would be helpful to read about the encounter between Joseph and Potiphar's wife in Genesis 39 for reinforcement and encouragement that lust can be avoided. This offering can help a man stand strong in his spirit while his flesh is under attack. With this in mind, safeguards should be built into mentoring programs or any ministry where males and females interact by removing opportunity to transgress. Here are some proactive thoughts:

1. A mentor should not arbitrarily make a decision to make home visits alone; or make a habit of responding to midnight "emergency" calls, texts or emails.

2. Whenever possible meet the family member of the opposite sex at church and in the company of another person affiliated with the mentoring program, or on the ministerial staff.

3. Immediately report any advances (flirting), suggestive conversations or solicitations (proposition) that will cause confusion, embarrassment, shame and pain to the child, mentoring program, church and the involved families (including the mentor's).

4. If you know that you know you are incapable of handling a particular relationship or you are too weak to fight an attraction on a professional and spiritual level please don't "test" yourself by trying.

5. Keep the ultimate goal in mind and that is the well-being and healthy growth and development of the mentee and not satisfying flesh.

The Rescue Paradox has snared men and women and has had ruinous consequences. Like most things in life if an action starts out wrong there is a greater probability that it will end up very wrong. Single mentors, under no circumstance, have the right to use mentoring as a "cover" to get sexually involved with single, separated, married, or divorced women. A married mentor or mother should not use mentoring as a cloak to mask an affair, no matter how desperate, lonely, or careful you think you are in avoiding detection. God sees all and so does someone else in the house; namely the mentee and any other children present.

Page | 306

Questions To Ponder

1. What steps have you taken to avoid the mentor's rescue paradox?

2. What feelings might a child experience caught in the middle of an illicit affair with his mom and mentor?

3. What would you say to a fellow mentor currently caught up in the rescue paradox?

Rescue Paradox Part Two

Pedophilia

The Penn State pedophile scandal broke as this book was being written. As the author and protector of children it would not have been authentic to my call to keep silent on this issue. Especially since the purpose of this book is geared to men called to lead, teach and nurture young men and boys. Pedophilia (adults that rape children) is an ultimate breach of trust. It must not be sanctioned, winked at, glossed over, or, God forbid, swept under the proverbial rug. Pedophiles can be found anywhere. They are in higher education and in dingy basements. They are educated and uneducated. They are white collar, blue collar and some wear a cleric's collar. Pedophiles can be super rich or very poor. They can be a father raping their own children or only having sex with other father's children. A pedophile has the ability to spot vulnerable youth and use their power, prestige, position, guile or brute force to rape a child.

Here are some other general characteristics of pedophiles taken from an online website:

1. Unusual interest or fascination with children.

2. Adult makes exaggerated claims about the sanctity of children, their purity, innocence, God sent, cuddly etc...

3. A pedophile will generally reveal his true nature the more comfortable he becomes in his surrounding because this is who he really is and is difficult to hide over a stretch of time.

4. Pedophiles are generally [operative word generally] over 30 years of age.

5. Child predators usually have ongoing problems making friends in their same peer group. They tend to be loners.

6.   Predators find ways to "legally" be around children and will cultivate a child over the course of weeks, months or years.

7.   Their methods are fairly simple-think of a courtship using gifts, flattery, attention, touching (a favorite trick is tickling), rubbing, fondling, kissing etc.

8.   Molesters of children are often time (not all the time) creepy - not to be confused with being quirky.

Pedophiles never think about the aftermath of their despicable deeds. They take what does not belong to them with impunity. The same child's pureness they endlessly extol is now forever sullied by their reprehensible act. This child stalker rushes off while covering his/her tracks until the next victim is sighted. Willie Sutton the infamous bank robber was asked why he robbed banks? His simple reply, "Because that's where the money is!" That is why pedophiles hang around scouting programs, houses of worship, athletic programs and mentoring programs, for the same reason Willie Sutton gave - that is where children are. Here are some thoughts how programs bringing men and boys together can make it difficult for pedophiles to operate:

1. Talk to parents and youth during orientation about program guidelines with a focus on what to do if a mentor makes remarks or takes actions that are inconsistent with the ethos of the program, church or parental rules and expectations.

2. Plan group trips with mentees and mentors as much as possible. If there are one-on-one day trips planned the venue must be vetted by leaders of the mentoring program and approved by a parent/guardian.

3. Mentors should be fingerprinted mainly to ascertain if there have been prior charges of pedophilia or sexual assault in their background. This is not to say that people can't change, but if this charge is "discovered" rather than revealed that is cause for a big red flag.

4. Parents should monitor Internet use in the home since predators are going online. Email exchanges between mentor and mentees should be preapproved and scrutinized by mentoring staff and parent(s).

5. Be wary of lavish gifts given to a child especially if no occasion justifies a gift.

6. A mentee should never be given permission to accompany a man on overnight trips that are not sanctioned by the mentoring program and properly chaperoned by mentoring staff. With that said a

mentor and mentee should NEVER stay in the same room.

MENTOR'S SPIRITUAL REFLECTION
STAIN OF SHAME

Who is a God like you, who pardons sin and forgives the transgressions of the remnant of his inheritance? You do not stay angry forever but delight to show mercy. You will again have compassion on us; you will tread our sins underfoot and hurl all of our iniquities into the depths of the sea.
Micah 7:18-19

It would be difficult to find a man who has not felt shame at some point in their lives (before or after being saved). This statement is ironic because we live in a time where seemingly there is no shame. People willingly write tell-all-books, "accidentally" release sex tapes and the like. They excitedly broadcast their most salacious private behavior on Facebook, YouTube or Tweet things that in another time would have surely brought shame. The desire to be famous, no matter the cost, has turned gossip into big business, linking shamelessness with fame and fortune - no matter how transitory or derogatory.

Some words that define shame are: humiliated, debased, mortified, embarrassed or disgraced. These are not good feelings to have especially when a person wants to appear stain free. Let's descend into the dark basement of life to search for brothers tainted by shame. He fears that personal secrets, if revealed, will expose him or family/loved ones to malicious gossip, hurtful ridicule or intrusive speculation.

It should be made clear that while we may all experience shame, most people, outside of the aforementioned Hollywood crowd and tag-a-long wannabes, find it difficult to talk about shame. The proper ethos of the church, to live upright before God, may have unintended consequences when otherwise saved, sanctified and Holy Ghost filled men are reticent to confess troubling secrets for fear of being sanctimoniously exposed, unfairly judged or callously ostracized. Shame builds its own nagging, never-ending, negative mental tautology (think of a hamster running on a treadmill day and night ending in the same place) that painfully saps the shame-ridden individual's self-esteem, personal strength and spiritual will.

Imagine being sold out for Christ and the stain of shame diminishes who you are; forcing you to manufacture an over the top 'Too Blessed To Be Stressed and Much Too Highly Favored' persona even though your sad eyes tell a much different story. Shame can emanate from an act committed at any time but the stain of shame can linger for a lifetime. Shame can come from a 'wayward' act done by a person in your family that smeared your family's 'good name'. Shame is like a caustic acid, the longer it lingers the more it corrodes. The longer it corrodes the harder the repair. Let's go to the scripture and see what we can learn to help men trying to expunge the stain of shame.

If we searched for a person to study in the Bible that had to deal with shame we should look no further than David. We could point to his son Absalom trying to usurp his power and seize the throne. Or we could look at David's other son raping his half-sister Tamar. These are horrid examples of how families can bring shame. The staining shameful act committed by David happened when he stole another man's wife, then set up the husband (Uriah The Hittite) to be sent to the front line where he was ultimately killed. David went on to father a child with the dead man's wife Bathsheba. Yes, David went through and suffered for his actions because shame causes pain. Hear David's timeless words of angst:

I am worn out calling for help, my throat is parched. My eyes fail, looking for my God. I am forced to restore what I did not steal. Rescue me from the mire, do not let me sink. Come near and rescue me; redeem me because of my foes. You know how I am scorned, disgraced and shamed; all of my enemies are before you. Scorn has broken my heart and left me helpless; I looked for sympathy and there was none, for comforters, but I found none. I am in pain and distress... Psalm 69:3, 4a, 14b, 18-20, 29a

If the truth be told all of us, including the young people we mentor, their friends or perhaps even their family members may harbor shame or carry the stain of shame. If a "shameful" secret is revealed or discovered during the mentor/mentee relationship here are some ways a mentor can effectively respond:

1. This is not the time to be judgmental; this also means exercising ultimate discipline and control over the urge to lift even an eyebrow in shock or surprise. If the person opening up senses that he is being judged then he will shut down and burrow deeper in his pain.

2. Don't minimize a person's feelings of shame by saying words like: "Is that all that is bothering you, I have done far worse?!" Or saying, "Just wait a while you'll get over it" and then switch the subject. This may make the hearer feel better but does absolutely nothing for the sharer.

3. Don't be too quick to apply a 'faith-fix.' There will be time for scriptures and prayer. When a person makes the decision to share a deep and hurtful pain- the ground one stands on is instantly transformed into holy ground. The best thing to do while

standing your ground is to empathetically listen to the person as he speaks his pain.

4. NEVER under any circumstance violate a person's expressed or expectation of confidentiality by sharing private matters to people who have no stake, no interest or no skills to address the situation.

Questions to Ponder

1. If you could unburden yourself of an act that causes you shame what would you identify?

2. Have you ever helped another man deal with his shame? If so how did it make you feel?

3. What would you say are the top three reasons men opt to keep the stain of shame to themselves?

MENTOR'S MISSION FUEL
MEN DEALING WITH ANGER AND LEARNING TO FORGIVE

Anger, when negative, volatile and unchecked, can be destructive to the object of the anger as well as harmful to the person who holds anger. Anger turned inward can manifest as depression. It is important to note that anger can also create opportunities for positive acts. For example, a person angry about the condition of a vacant lot decides to clean it up. The focus of our sharing is centered on anger that interferes with a man's quality of life and is dangerous to him and others. Here are trigger issues culled from a men's retreat responding to the question-what makes you angry:

- **ANGRY AT SELF**—Brothers mentioned they know they made mistakes in the past and can't shake their anger. One could imagine that different situations could trigger anger in a way that is disproportionate to the actual situation or encounter. It is easy to say, "Let go and let God." What is important to figure out is the answer to this question: Is anger holding you, or are you holding on to anger?

- **ANGRY AT FAMILY**—There were many responses that dealt with anger toward a family member. Pain suffered at the hands of kin runs exceptionally deep. When the person who is supposed to love you and be there for you turns against you in either thought, word or deed, it hurts and that hurt can cause lasting anger, pain and separation.

- **ANGRY DUE TO A SITUATION**—Several brothers mentioned questionable police shootings that reinforce their anger at the system. Situational anger engendered by systemic causes is hard to deal with because it is not necessarily directed at a person. It is impossible to sit down with the system co-workers/supervisors that provoked angry responses and have a clarifying talk. One young man mentioned a death of a friend that has caused pent-up anger in him.

Forgiveness is a process and not an act. Forgiveness of self and others can eradicate most forms of caustic anger. Jonah was angry with God and his short book ends with him remaining angry. Imagine being angry for the rest of your life. Some people are held in the clutch of anger by people who have departed this world yet they *haunt* the memory of the living. Men, know that you can serve God and be angry-that is your right (even if you are wrong). You should also know that if you do so you will live beneath your privilege. Here are some scripture references that can be used to help the process of forgiveness:

For if you forgive men when they sin against you, your heavenly Father will also forgive you. But if you do not forgive men their sins, your heavenly Father will not forgive you. Matthew 6:14-15

Then Peter came to Jesus and asked, "Lord how many times should I forgive my brother when he sins against me? Up to seven times?" Jesus answered, "I tell you, not seven times, but seventy-seven times." Matthew 18:21- 22

"If your brother sins, rebuke him and if he repents forgive him. If he sins against you seven times in a day, and seven times comes back to you and say, 'I repent,' forgive him." Luke 17: 3b-4

Get rid of all bitterness, rage and anger, brawling and slander, along with every form of malice. Be kind and compassionate to one another, forgiving each other, just as Christ forgave you. Ephesians 4:31-32

So the question and challenge to you is: Do you want to get rid of anger that has diminished your life and the life of others around you? If so, then forgive. Forgive yourself. Forgive others. Ask for forgiveness from God. Forgiveness is not a sign of weakness or necessarily an admission of guilt. It is a definitive statement of readiness to move on with life.

Questions to Ponder

1. Can you recall a time when your anger got in the way and could have or did have serious consequence?

2. What ways have you learned to control your anger?

3. Can you name a time when you were able to productively use anger to address a situation or person?

MENTOR'S TESTIMONY
A FATHERLESS GENERATION: LIVING WITHOUT A MENTOR
By David Ramos

Rev. David Ramos is a minister and the administrator of a bible school in New Jersey. He is the Founder and Facilitator of the Latino Leadership Circle and the developer of the ACTS Urban Youth Leadership Program that presently runs in three states. David is a trainer and conference speaker; he conducts workshops and conferences for pastors globally. Rev. Ramos received his Master of Divinity from Princeton Theological Seminary and his Master of Social Work from Rutgers University. His interests are in education, pastoral care, urban and youth ministries, globalization, and public policy. He and his wife live in New Jersey.

When I was in the eighth grade I learned the word "mentor" and began to long for one. I remember watching old films where fathers took their sons fishing and somehow internalized that this was some kind of rite of passage between fathers and sons. Television displayed idyllic scenes of patient, wise and understanding fathers who deposited wisdom and character building lessons to appreciative sons. My own journey with my father was a painful one. My father was *not* a drunkard, a womanizer, nor did he ever curse around us. On the contrary he was an extremely responsible man, who was an excellent provider. He worked two jobs. He was a homeowner and proudly owned the nicest car on the block. However, years of working the sugar cane fields in Puerto Rico, then working in a factory in New Jersey, had taken its toll. He was gruff and always seemed to be angry about something. He was defiant and seemed to possess a streak of sadism.

As I grew up I too became defiant and found my place on the streets of Brooklyn, those mean streets became my playground, my school, my escape, my fix, and my adventure. I hated being at home and was constantly on the streets. I remember one day a girlfriend gave me the song *"Street Life"* by Randy Crawford as a gift because she said it reminded her of me. I privately took offense at the time, but this began to make me question my life on the streets. Time would go by and one day, I surrendered my life to Jesus on those same streets. I am a product of street evangelism from those "crazy folk" many are fond of criticizing. I entered a discipleship program and I remembered that word I learned -*"mentor"* and began to pray for one.

Then one day, I came across a verse and felt I received an answer - but it wasn't the one I expected. In Proverbs 6:6— 8 it said, *"Go to the ant, you sluggard; consider its ways, and be wise! It has no commander, no overseer, or ruler, yet it stores its provisions in summer and gathers its food at harvest."*

What I had interpreted at this time was a kind of rebuke and in it I felt God was telling me, *"You do not need a mentor, I'll be your mentor!"* I said, *"Okay, God,"* and since then I have lived without a mentor with perhaps one exception of a brief season in my life. Little did I know how prophetic this verse would be, but how lonely and painful the path of ministry would be for me, and how the salvation I encountered truly depended upon my understanding of a God that loved me and would never give up on me - even when it seemed that those around me conspired against me.

There were so many moments in my life that the places that should have been safe spaces became rife with danger; the people who should have cared for me were the ones who hurt me, and those who should have opened doors were the ones who shut them in my face. Time would not allow me to relate experiences of betrayal, jealousy, contention, lies, subterfuge, competition, hatred, marginalization, oppression, etc. Welcome to the human side of ministry!

Living without a mentor may be difficult but living with a one that does not have your [best] interests in mind can be worse. While having been hurt by leaders, I've learned to trust in God, I've developed a heart of compassion to assist the emerging generation of leaders so that they will not have to suffer the things I suffered. I've learned to seek the rainbow when it rains, and to truly appreciate those that love me. Many pastors, for whom I have been a pastor to, tell me that I have a father's spirit; this has truly blessed me because as someone who feels fatherless, and not ever having a true mentor, I have become a father and mentor to others.

I've learned to appreciate every ounce of encouragement I can find in life and I still rejoice in spending intimate time with a God who has been loving, kind, merciful, faithful father, and yes - the best mentor anyone can possible hope for! My prayer is that these lessons can somehow help and/or inspire those for whom at this moment in life are living without a mentor.

CHAPTER SIXTEEN

MENTOR'S CODE OF ETHICS

Trust in the LORD with all your heart and lean not to your own understanding; in all your ways acknowledge him and he will make your paths straight. Proverbs 3:5-6

This book started off talking about the high calling of mentors of faith. I have worked for secular nonprofit agencies where there were multiple levels of accountability. It would be great if workers always allowed their thoughts, words and deeds to be governed by high standards not because they are being paid but because that is the demand they place on themselves. I recall telling my staff that the agency can't pay me enough to give what is in my heart to freely share. A true professional has a defined sense of accountability, is guided by a vision set by a moral compass and will work in and out of season. It should also be said that this person, unfortunately, is a rare find.

I learned while working in inner-city youth programs and while running a high school that young people are always watching adults. I also learned there are no secrets. Everybody, young and old, has a best friend to share their secrets. I still wince when I think about a male staff member who took advantage of an all-too-willing teenager who some said really trapped him. This act almost toppled an effective program by hobbling our best effort to save lives. This is one reason why it is imperative that mentors hold themselves and their peers to a high ethical code of conduct. It is not acceptable to be a mentor and have a relationship that you must hide from your wife, fellow mentors, pastor or the Lord. Protecting and projecting a strong, positive character is essential if transformative change in self and mentees is the real goal.

Please allow me to paraphrase President Abraham Lincoln when I say, 'You can fool some of the people all of the time but you can't fool all of the people all of the time'. When you fool yourself into believing you are something that you are not and compound this act by trying to fool God, you are indeed a hopeless and unethical fool. Here are Bible-based principles for developing the ethical, moral and spiritual character of mentors prepared by the Holy Spirit to provide examples of learning, leading and living to young people.

1. *We love because He first loved us. If anyone says, "He loves God," yet hates his brother, he is a liar. For anyone who does not love his brother whom he has seen cannot love God whom he has not seen. And he has given us this command: Whoever loves God must also love his brother. 1John 4:19-21*

2. *Let the little children come unto me and do not hinder them, for the kingdom of God belongs to such as these. I tell you the truth, anyone who will not receive the kingdom of God like a little child will never enter it." Luke 18:16b-17*

3. *Jesus said to his disciples: "Things that cause people to sin are bound to come, but woe to the person through whom they come. It would be better for him to be thrown in the sea with a millstone tied around his neck than for him to cause one of these little ones to sin. So watch yourselves. Luke 17: 1-3*

4. *If you hold to my teaching, you are really my disciples. Then you will know the truth and the truth shall set you free. John 8:31b-32*

5. *To the elders among you, I appeal as a fellow elder...Serving as overseers—not because you must, but because you are willing as God wants you to be; not greedy for money, but eager to serve, not lording it over those entrusted to you, but being examples to the flock. 1Peter 5:1a-3*

6. *But you, dear friends, build yourselves up in your most holy faith, and pray in the Holy Spirit. Keep yourselves in God's love as you wait for the mercy of our Lord Jesus Christ to bring you to eternal life. Be merciful to those who doubt: snatch others from the fire and save them; to others show mercy,*

mixed with fear - hating even the clothing stained by corrupted flesh. Jude 1:20-23

7. *Do not merely listen to the word and so deceive yourselves. Do what it says. Anyone who listens to the word but does not do what it says is like a man who looks at his face in the mirror, and after looking at himself goes away and immediately forgets what he looks like. But the man who looks intently at the perfect law that gives freedom, and continues to do this, not forgetting what he has heard, but doing it - he will be blessed in what he does. If anyone considers himself religious and yet does not keep a tight rein on his tongue, he deceives himself and his religion is worthless.*
James 1:22-26

8. *If anyone thinks he is something when he is nothing, he deceives himself. Each one should test his own actions. Then he can take pride in himself, without comparing himself to somebody else, for each one should carry his own load.*
Galatians 6: 3-5

9. *You have heard me teach many things that have been confirmed by many reliable witnesses. Teach*

these great truths to trustworthy people who are able to pass them on to others.
2 Timothy 2:2

Questions to Ponder

1. Which scripture best captures what you are striving to project to self and to others?

2. Which scripture represents your mind/spirit struggle?

3. What scripture(s) would you add to round out this list?

MENTOR'S SPIRITUAL REFLECTION
A LESSON IN MAJESTIC HUMILITY
John 13: 1-17

Brothers, what comes to mind when you think about the word humility? Humility—the word euphoniously rolls out of the mouth-H.U.M.I.L.I.T.Y. But I caution you, while humility is easy to say and hear, humility is hard to fully comprehend and put into practice. According to The American Heritage Dictionary, some common synonyms for humility are: meek, modest, lowly and deferentially respectful. All dictionaries define words according to the most common usage to the least common use.

How do you define humility as it relates to the two you's - the you you try to be and the real you? Are you meek? Are you modest? Are you lowly? Are you deferentially respectful? Now don't get nervous if you come up a little weak in any category, or closer to the truth, if you come on too strong as far as having humility goes. The Lord has deemed that we all need a refresher course in humility. There are many reasons that men reject humility as a mode of behavior. Men are taught from an early age that if you submit it means you're a loser.

While looking for a definition of humility, I gazed one word up and saw humiliation. I believe some brothers in and out of the church don't want any part of humility because they think it automatically leads to humiliation! Some men honestly believe if you are humble, meek, lowly, and deferentially respectful that you are really weak and that you have low self-esteem essentially saying to the world, 'I am your doormat'. That is why some people find it hard to submit.

While other people may think if you submit it means that you were wrong, that you are not strong enough to fight for your convictions. There are some brothers who are power drunk and will never willingly trade the power benefits of always being right for the seemingly ascetic principles consistent with humility, mainly admitting that you were wrong and God forbid, apologize. These men would rather practice the flesh-driven art of humiliation rather than practice the discipline of humility. Their underlying principle is: humiliate before being humiliated! So are you ready for a much needed Lesson in Majestic Humility? Let's go to the text.

Jesus has assembled his disciples just before the Passover. The entire party is seated in preparation to eat. Before the table was spread, before grace could be said, Jesus did yet another mind-blowing act that is missed by the deep and shallow alike. Now it would be fair to ask: what could be more remarkable than Jesus saying, "Peace be still" to the wind and the waves and be obeyed, or walking on water? What could be more mind-blowing than speaking life to a dead man named Lazarus and he comes back to life? The game-changing event that I am referring to was not predicated on some unobservable supernatural miracle performed by Jesus, but on an observable natural happening.

Sometimes it is not deep. I am talking about an act that even tongue talking saints still do not fully comprehend or can operationalize. I am talking about Jesus' demonstration of Majestic Humility. Take a peek with your natural eyes, but discern with spiritual sensibility Majestic Humility in action. As shown in the text: Jesus took off his robe, tied a towel around his waist and was about to wash the feet of the disciples. He was going to wash the feet of his followers… those who sat at his feet. He was going to wash the feet of men who were: weak, unfocused, an extorter, a doubter, a curser and one who would betray Him.

To grasp the significance of this pericope, you have to know that it was customary in that time for travelers to have their feet washed when they entered a house as a sign of hospitality. This common courtesy, extended to guests, always fell upon the lowest person in the household. And that person was usually a slave. Now look at Jesus through spiritual eyes as he is about to bow at the feet of the disciples. Satan could not force him to bow down, but he willingly submits to people like you and me. Can you see him bending down with the towel wrapped securely around his waist? Jesus did not ask for permission to wear the towel. Jesus did not call a board meeting to see what the higher up thought about him wearing the towel. He did not ring up the Bishop nor take an opinion poll from the Pharisees or Sadducees to see if tying the towel around his waist was appropriate. Jesus knew who he was; where he came from and where he would soon return.

When Jesus was about to wash Peter's feet he rebuffed Jesus' attempt. Peter did not see the magnanimity of this act. He did not see Majestic Humility, he could only see humiliation. Peter probably asked, 'How could the Lord of Lord's, the King of King's, the one I confessed to be the Christ wash my feet?' People already are confused about

Jesus saying he is not the Messiah. Some say he is a prophet; or a deluded carpenter's son. Why would Jesus add to the drama by adding to the confusion? Why would he wash our feet?'

It was at this point that Jesus gave Peter and the world a 'King of King-sized' lesson in Majestic Humility. He told Peter, "Unless I wash your feet, you have no part of me." Jesus knew that humility had to be more than an intellectual concept, because so many people would be happy to think they were acting with humility rather than with impunity. Jesus wanted to demonstrate that humility had to be earned through service to others. Are you hearing me? After today, you can no longer think that you possess Majestic Humility and yet refuse to mentor youth, feed the hungry, clothe the naked, help the widow, visit the prisoner, in short, help the least of these among us. So brothers, it is time for your advanced lesson in Majestic Humility as taught through the scriptures by the great and humble practitioner Jesus:

Matthew 20:28a—The Son of Man did not come to be served but to serve.

Matthew 11:29a—Take my yoke upon you and learn of me for I am gentle and humble in heart.

Mark 9:35b—If anyone wants to be first, he must be the very last and the servant of all.

If you want to be a practitioner and teacher of Majestic Humility you can no longer be content merely choosing to serve when convenient or when you feel you have no other choice. You have to know that you are called to serve! Peter had to come to this same conclusion, not through a cognitive change, but a radical transformation deep in his soul. Look at what Peter said after the Holy Ghost elevated and lowered him at the same time:

Live as free men, but do not use your freedom as a cover-up for evil. Live as servants of God. Show proper respect to everyone. Love the brotherhood of believers and fear God. 1Peter 2:10

If you are saved, if you know that you are called, anointed, appointed and expected to be a servant; or if you know that you should be doing more to serve, it does not matter. You can serve others with Majestic Humility. Don't be afraid. Don't worry about appearing weak. Jesus said that his strength is masked as weakness. And don't concern yourself with thoughts of humiliation.

The world tried to use the cross as a symbol of humiliation for Jesus. He was able to make the despised cross, the very symbol of humiliation, into an everlasting symbol of mental, physical and spiritual liberation. Jesus voluntarily lowered himself so that one day you and I could be raised up. Jesus was sacrificed so that we could have life and have it more abundantly. He showed us that it was possible to love our enemies. Jesus sent the Holy Spirit: the enabler, the comforter, the teacher and the attitude adjuster. When you add it all up my brothers the sum total equals Majestic Humility!

MENTOR'S MISSION FUEL
ARE YOU A BE BACK BROTHER?

I remember calling my mentee Shawn Dove and asking him what does I Got Your Back, mean to him? He replied, "Do you remember what you felt back in the day when a brother said, "Don't worry, I got your back?" I smiled after recalling the meaning behind this 'ole school' street pledge that no matter who, what, when, or where, the vow giver would stand by his word to protect you. We both laughed, but probably wanted to cry because of the growing number of struggling men (and boys) who never hear, 'my brother, don't worry, I got your back'.

Let me take this to another level. Some of you may be familiar with the parable of The Good Samaritan. Just in case you are a tad hazy, allow me to offer this modern version of the story:

A brother on his way home from the check cashing spot one late Friday was dragged in a dark alley and jacked for his money. A stranger passed by and his fear would not allow him to intervene. Another man stopped, looked and felt pity for the brother but left because he did not have time to get involved. A third brother passed by and heard moans coming from the alley. Without hesitation, he comforted the injured man and called for help. The good brother followed up days later and found out that the badly injured man would need time to heal (he lost his job at the car wash after the robbery). He gave money to the injured brother's wife so she could feed their children and pay the rent. He said to the sobbing pair that he would be back next week to take care of any loose ends.

The take away point from this urban parable is that the helper did not know the brother or his family, but intervened nevertheless and kept his word to return thereby earning the honor of being called 'Be Back Brother'. A Be Back Brother (BBB) is inner-directed to help others by giving either, time, talent or treasure. A Be Back Brother's word is his bond (do you remember back in the day saying my word is bond?).

It is clear that we need strong, focused and spirit-fueled Be Back Brothers to step up to the plate. There are many unmet needs in our churches, families and communities. Allow me to make some suggestions where strategic BBB intervention can make a difference in the lives of young men.

- We need BBB mentors to help others successfully crack the man code. This can be done informally (helping a single mom's son) or formally through scouting or a program like AMACHI (mentor children of incarcerated parents) or Rite of Passage Programs like Blue Nile and Sons of Promise.

- There are many local youth development programs struggling to keep their doors open while fighting to keep young people safe. A BBB group could adopt a youth agency and do the following: raise operating cash, create scholarships, join Board of Directors, or share "secrets" of success with young people through rap groups, career days and the like.

- Identify other BBB who can open doors to the world of work through job shadowing (invite youth to your job), internships or employment. The group could fund a youth job line given to a house of worship, a community agency or administered directly.

Unfortunately, fathers well beyond their teen years, struggling with parental or custodial obligations have been summarily written off as no good worthless dead-beat dads. It must be said that there are brothers who are quite happy being serial baby dads and could care less. However, there are men who need and want help to do right for their families. I believe my calling is to encourage concerned BBB to get together, stand together and work together on behalf of fathers of all ages and circumstances who need to hear, "I got your back."

Do you ignore brothers in need like the first man in the parable? The second brother shows that feelings unattached to action are a waste of time and emotion. If you know down in the marrow of your being that you are called to be a Be Back Brother, you are free to move in the great power that enables you to live this truth: I am my brother's keeper, friend, resource, motivator and guide. My fellow BBB, go forth and do good works with bold determination. Always remember that God got your back.

MENTOR'S TESTIMONY

REDEEMING TIME
By Richard Buery J. D.

In October 2009, Richard R. Buery, Jr. was named the tenth President and Chief Executive Officer of The Children's Aid Society. He is the first black leader of

Children's Aid and the youngest since Charles Loring Brace founded the agency in 1853. Children's Aid is an independent, not-for-profit organization established to help children in poverty to succeed and thrive. Children's Aid serves 70,000 children in New York City and around the country each year through a network of services and programs that support children and their families from before birth through young adulthood. While still an undergraduate at Harvard, he co-founded the Mission Hill Summer Program, an enrichment program for children in the Mission Hill Housing Development in the Roxbury section of Boston. More recently, he co-founded and served as executive director of iMentor, a technology education and mentoring program that each year connects New York City middle and high school students with professional mentors through on-line and face-to-face meetings. Already one of the largest youth mentoring organizations in New York City, iMentor is currently undergoing a national expansion. A graduate of Harvard College and the Yale Law School, Mr. Buery has a background in law, education, and politics. He has been named one of Ebony Magazine's Thirty Leaders of the Future under Thirty, one of Crain's New York Business' 40 Leaders of the Future under 40, one of the grio.com's 100 African American leaders, and one of the Root 100 black leaders. He has also received the Mary McLeod Bethune

Recognition Award from the National Council of Negro Women; the Extraordinary Black Man Award for Humanitarianism from the United Negro College Fund, and the inaugural outstanding alumnus award from the Phillips Brooks House Association at Harvard University.

There is an old, great, true quote: "Time is more valuable than money. You can get more money, but you cannot get more time." Certainly in my own life, time seems the most precious of commodities – time for work, for family, for friends, for me, always seems in short supply. Yet, throughout my professional life, I have been amazed how frequently others have made time for me. Thirteen years ago, my friend Matt Klein and I were hired by John Griffin to lead a start-up called iMentor. The idea was simple but powerful. Research demonstrates that a quality, long-term one-on-one mentoring relationship can have a tremendous impact on young people. Youth in mentoring programs perform better in school and are more likely to avoid high-risk behaviors like drug use and delinquency. Yet, throughout the country, there are millions of young people who are in need of mentors – indeed one study showed that 17.5 million youth nationwide are at high need for mentoring.

While 44 million Americans say they would consider mentoring a child, only 3 million actually do so. There are many reasons for this gap between those who say they will consider mentoring and those who actually do so; and between the 17.5 million or more children who need mentors and the 3 million who step up to serve. One of the biggest reasons is time. Too many busy, working adults don't believe they have the time to give. iMentor leverages the Internet to reduce that barrier. iMentor volunteers meet their mentees in person once a month, but communicate regularly through email. By reducing the time volunteers have to spend traveling every weekend to see their mentees, iMentor has been able to dramatically expand the ranks of volunteer mentors: indeed, 70% of iMentor volunteers are first time mentors.

I was 27 when we started iMentor, and I have thought many times since that the hardest part of being the boss – by far – is not having a boss. I have been envious of those friends and colleagues who spoke with admiration of the bosses they have had who contributed to their careers and personal growth. As the director of a youth mentoring organization, the answer for me was obvious. In addition to recruiting mentors for the children we served, I got in the business of recruiting mentors for myself; mentors who could coach me on the challenges of recruiting and managing staff, raising money, balancing work and life, and making difficult decisions. Mentors who would answer my questions, challenge my preconceptions, or confirm my instincts. Some of these mentors came from the world of business, like John. Others have been friends and peers like Matt.

They have included giants in the fields of education and youth development, like the Rev. Dr. Alfonso Wyatt and Dr. Michael Carrera, a leader in the fight against adolescent pregnancy, who would become my colleague at the Children's Aid Society when I took over as President and CEO three years ago. These people have all been instrumental in my personal and professional development. I have always been struck by how open and generous people have been with their time – even in the earliest days of my career when we were getting iMentor off the ground and none of the people I reached out to knew who I was. I have been known to pick up the phone and cold call some leader I admired, and ask if they would be willing to spend some mentoring time with me. In over a decade, I can't recall anyone ever saying no.

These gifts of time are precious. And I have tried to pay them forward by offering my time to those just beginning careers as teachers, social entrepreneurs, social workers, counselors or youth development professionals. This is to the chagrin of my assistant who has the unenviable task of managing my often crazy schedule. But how can I ask others to volunteer their time in service if I am not willing to do the same? And what better way to express my thanks to my many mentors by sharing my time with others?

CHAPTER 17

MENTORING SISTERS MESSAGE TO MEN

Does not wisdom call out? Does not understanding raise her voice? "To you, O men, I call out; I raise my voice to all mankind..." Proverbs: 8:1,4

I have the privilege of meeting strong, progressive and spirit-minded sisters who are national leaders in mentoring, entrepreneurs, education, ministry and writing to and about black men and boys. It became clear to me as I got closer to finishing this book that it was important for the voice of committed sisters in struggle to be heard. So I present five dear friends, mentees and colleagues who graciously agreed to contribute their insight and passion to this work.

REFLECTIONS ON A JOURNEY TOWARDS MENTORING

By Rev. Dr. Mariah Britton

Dr. Mariah Britton is founder and CEO of the Moriah Institute, a new non-profit dedicated to youth development through rites of passage and at building collaborations in the area of comprehensive sexuality education with seminaries. She holds a Master's of Divinity degree from Union Theological Seminary and recently completed the doctoral program at New York University, focusing on family marriage and human sexuality. Dr. Britton was the Youth Pastor at Riverside Church and she currently teaches at Drew Theological School.

When I was a teen, I don't think my parents really understood what was happening in the world in quite the same way that I did. I came of age in an era in which civil rights for black people was part of the conversation in the adult world and the subsequent explosion of racial pride, combined with a strong sense of change and new possibility was in the atmosphere. As a budding poet I was completely in love with words, meaning suggestion and the power of metaphor. I was introduced to a multiverse of black writers, jazz, art and bodacious indignation for how black people were treated in America.

These were not things I could talk about with my parents or my siblings for that matter. I don't think it was because they didn't care but were focused on the day to day drive for survival, keeping their kids safe from "the streets" and providing a decent home. Talk about cultural issues did not happen in the Bible Study I attended at the Methodist Church.

But thank God for James Weldon Johnson Community Center and Benjamin Franklin High School. In both places were teachers and counselors, who when I think about today, were only just a few years older than us teens, who were dedicated to their work, creative in their approach to youth development and who communicated trust and hope in us. With one teacher in particular, who was a writer, our time together was more like an apprenticeship, there was a language and energy that was unique; it helped me to listen for that special "beat of my internal drummer." It introduced me to the skill of sharing language, meaning and feeling; perhaps there was a bit of imitating his style in the beginning; but imitation is the first order of exchange in training; as a mentor he helped me to hone my talent in a particular discipline. Soon my own voice materialized on the page and in spoken word. I felt this in the many writing workshops I participated in years later.

Looking at the work I do today as a leader of a Rites of Passage program for youth in grades 10 – 12, I know that my own experience of being mentored has greatly influenced my decision to work with youth. In fact, before I left high school I knew I wanted to work with teens because I felt the impact teachers and other youth workers can have. Over the years I have taught high school, led summer day camp, organized youth ministries and have led courses in seminaries for people who want to work with youth. All of this stems from my early experience of being mentored. In the New Testament letter to the Hebrews it is said *"faith is the substance of things hoped for and the evidence of things not seen."* This speaks to how a mentor is engaged with the person she/he works with. It is not yet evident of what is inside a young person so one speaks to the potential, with faith that God has already planted within the mentee something we are to draw out of them. Mentoring acknowledges the humanity of the fledgling; it recognizes that the person before them has something precious to offer the world that simply needs time, coaxing and patience to blossom.

I also believe that mentoring is a practice of harvesting the pandemonium that occasions all of our lives. Sometimes teens do things because they are curious, sometimes because they like the feel of something that is risky or dangerous, sometimes because it just feels good to do a thing and sometimes they are just trying on a new idea. I also know that teens may be trying to shock or unnerve the adults in their lives but many times a teen simply does not know why they do a thing or say a thing. It just comes out or it remains inside them because they feel so many things at the same time it is difficult to sort them out with coherent communication. They experience a terrible sense of chaos but out of that confusion can, if in the presence of a caring mentor, emerge beauty and intelligence, unprecedented wisdom and courage that can heal the world.

Some of my most rewarding experiences in mentoring have been in situations where the teen seemed to be in such turmoil with family, friends, school but who was able to keep it together because there was a place to be where they could be safe, their ideas held in confidence and they were counseled to move towards the light in their lives. I think mentoring is about helping the mentee find the right light for their life. For many youth it is a matter of exposure to the light that will help them grow that light could be from a myriad of things - books, events, people, athletics, artistic expression, cooking, building, computers, plants, travel - and so many more.

For this reason, with the exception of acts of uncontrolled violence, I do my best to never turn a teen away from any of the programs I lead because you never know when the light is going to turn on. There is an old gospel tune *"shine on me, shine on me; let the light from the lighthouse shine on me."* Our task is to listen, observe and encourage trust enough so that a person is able to speak their truth find the light that will bless them from a deep place within. A light that will help them to understand they are on a journey and are not a fixed destination.

HURTING AND HEALING: REFLECTIONS ON MEN AND EMOTIONAL PAIN
By Zakiya Newland, Ph.D., LCSW

With a very clear desire to become a social worker, Dr. L. Zakiya Newland earned her BSW from Morgan State University, her MSW from the Graduate School of Social Service at Fordham University and her Ph.D. from the Wurzweiler School of Social Work at Yeshiva University. Dr. Newland's career was cultivated in Harlem, New York, where she practiced as a clinical social worker, community liaison, program developer and mental health clinic administrator. Dr. Newland is currently an Associate Professor in the Department of Social Work at Molloy College in Long Island. As a product of an urban environment, Dr. Newland has an awareness of and appreciation for intervention strategies that seek to empower various populations at the personal and political levels of their lives. In 2009, Dr. Newland established an innovative private practice, Educate 2 Elevate Consultation Services, which provides a range of clinical and administrative services. Dr. Newland is a NYS Licensed Clinical Social Worker and holds membership and leadership in several social work and professional organizations. Dr. Newland was selected by the Board of Directors of the National Association of Professional Women as the 2010/2011 Woman of the Year in the field of Counseling/Human Services

I am the youngest of three girls raised by my parents. Being raised in a female-dominated household led me to have a very narrow frame of reference for the development and condition of men. My father was a very present force in my life but in many ways, he was a mystery to me. Although we were connected there was a disconnect because at times, I misunderstood him. He was not the verbally expressive type and I can remember as a teenager questioning his commitment to us because of the things he didn't say. I began to wonder about his true feelings because I hardly heard them. I was measuring him by standards that represented a myopic view of expressing emotion. I was looking for words while he was consistently showing actions. It wasn't until adulthood when I realized he lived and loved through his actions, not his words.

During the week, he drove us to and picked us up from school. He spent his Saturdays driving us to dance class, then taking many of the neighborhood children to the local park and on Sunday, he worshipped and served faithfully at church. I witnessed his commitment to his Masonic organization and the tenant patrol of our housing development. He truly was a great man and I never had the opportunity to tell him because by the time I recognized the greatness, he was deceased. I wish I had the opportunity to tell him that I misunderstood his expressions of love and I'm sorry if I caused him emotional pain.

As a Licensed Clinical Social Worker in private practice, I have been exposed to many men whose emotional pain was unnoticed and misunderstood. Losing a job, home or vehicle can alter one's lifestyle, challenge one's self-concept and produce a considerable amount of distress. This pain is less likely to be misunderstood because it is connected to a situation. In some aspects of my work, there were times when the reason for the pain was hidden. Complaints of 'baby mama drama' disguised relational pain. Blaming the economy for difficulty finding employment revealed societal pain. Questioning one's purpose masked a faith crisis and led to spiritual pain. Family pain was at the root of cutting off communication with a relative and saying, 'he's dead to me'.

These real issues have caused real pain. Pain when a husband struggles with loving his wife through her depression. Pain when a father, who provides a high quality of life for his family, is disrespected by his young adult children. Pain when a man reconnects with his family and community after incarceration and worries about the one thing that he can't get back...time. Pain when discriminatory practices at work cause feelings of frustration. One man even stated that he just wanted therapy to have an opportunity to vent without any negative consequences so he could avoid the pain of people dismissing his feelings. These men initiated therapy for themselves as a way of acknowledging their emotional pain and the need for support, encouragement and validation. They made a commitment to embark on a healing journey.

Therapy is certainly not the road that many men will take in their healing journeys. Less formalized but equally impactful, mentoring provides another pathway. These supportive relationships develop and when trust and rapport are established, mentors can be 'let in' to the vulnerabilities that the men they are working with experience. Exposure to others' vulnerabilities can be a difficult dynamic to manage. The potential exists to feel overwhelmed and helpless. You may even feel consumed by the other person's issues. In extreme instances vicarious or secondary trauma can be experienced by the person desiring to offer an empathic response to emotional pain.

Therefore, it is important to consider your own viewpoints when encountering someone's brokenness. Do you have a support system and do you utilize it when needed? Are you comfortable with vulnerability? What are your views on men experiencing emotional pain? Would you make a referral to a mental health professional or spiritual counselor? Would you engage in a professional helping relationship?

In the spirit of 'keeping it real', let's acknowledge that emotional pain is real. The recent tragic death of Chris Lighty made the hip-hop generation pause and take notice. Facebook posts, tweets and blogs flooded social media bringing attention to depression and vulnerability. So as you mentor from the inside out, make a commitment to the concept of emotional wellness. Attend to the spoken and unspoken needs of the men you encounter. Take note of the presence of pain, obvious and hidden, and know that when the inner man is strengthened...the outer man will shine.

Warmly Submitted and In Honor of My Father,

BLACK PAIN: IT JUST LOOKS LIKE WE ARE NOT HURTING

By Terrie M. Williams

Reprinted by permission

Terrie M. Williams is a licensed clinical social worker with a BA in psychology and sociology from Brandeis University and an MS in social work from Columbia University. She is the founder of The Terrie Williams Agency, which is one of the country's most successful African- American public relations and communications firms, and has handled some of the biggest names in entertainment, sports, business and politics. Terrie Williams is also the founder of Stay Strong Foundation, with a mission to urge corporate and individual responsibility, and to offer educational and leadership workshops, internships, and mentoring opportunities for youth. She has also received countless honors and awards, including: The New York Women in Communications Matrix Award in Public Relations (she was the first woman of color to receive this award in its 70-year history); the PRSA New York Chapter's Phillip Dorf Mentoring Award; and The Citizen's Committee for New York Marietta Tree Award for Public Service. In 1996 she was the first person of color honored with the Vernon C. Schranz Distinguished Lectureship at Ball State University, and in 1998 she donated her papers to the Howard University Moorland-Springarn Research Center Archives Terrie Williams has launched the national mental health advocacy campaign "Healing Starts With Us." A best- selling author of four books including her latest, entitled BLACK PAIN: It Just Looks Like We Are Not Hurting (Scribner).

A depressed Black man doesn't necessarily look like he's "down in the dumps," "cryin' the blues," or any of the other clichés we use to describe what depression looks like. A depressed Black man might be the most energetic man you know, a ball of fire who never stops moving or doing, whether or not the moving gets him anywhere or the doing does anything. A depressed Black man might be accomplished in all kinds of socially acceptable areas (career, church, sports, school), or he might be the kind of man who can't stop making everything worse for himself and anyone who loves him. What most depressed men have in common, and depressed Black man in particular, is that they will do anything not to wind up sitting with unbearable feelings. That's why it's so often underlying depression: that unexplored and not talked about pain that underlies the destructive and self-destructive actions in the lives of way too many of our brothers. How many? Well, according to statistics, only 9 percent of men have suffered or will ever suffer from depression - but statistics are only just so accurate. They never tell more than a small part of the story.

In Terrence Real's powerful book on men and depression, *I Don't Want To Talk About It: Overcoming the Secret Legacy of Male Depression*, he argues, as I do, that men are suffering from depression at rates far higher than statistics show. When I look at our community and I see our brothers dying every day from violence or heart attacks or drugs or disease, or wasting the best years of their lives in prison, I know these men are not well in their souls. These men are not making suicidal choices because they've sat down and calmly reasoned it out; nobody has ever said, "I could go to school, have a career, make a decent living, marry a woman I love, and build a home and a family with her, but I've thought about it a lot and I know I'll be happier if I drop out, do drugs, sell drugs, gangbang, make babies I can't support, spend half my life in prison, or just get killed."

But when society (in the form of poor housing, non-real health care, unchecked crime, education barely worthy of the name, and welfare programs that are hard to get off) doesn't support those choices for those unlucky enough to be born into its urban poor - when it often works directly against the things we might think of as wise and humane choices - it shouldn't be a surprise that so many choose against their own best interests, against themselves, so many times a day, every day of the week. The truth is that these men are deeply depressed, so deeply they can't even name it. And the horror is that it's so secret they can't even tell themselves. So much of my drive to write this book comes from the belief, grounded in faith, that if I am not well, you are not well, and if you are not well, I am not well. Our brothers are not well, and something has to be done. We must help them name their pain so that they stop visiting denial, abuse, and destructiveness on themselves and those around them.

Excerpted from 'BLACK PAIN' by Terrie Williams (Scribner). 2008 by Terrie Williams.

DON'T FOCUS ON WHO'S HOLDING YOU BACK, INSTEAD FOCUS ON WHO'S WITH YOU AND WHO HAS SUCCESSFULLY GONE BEFORE YOU

By: Cassandra Mack, MSW

Cassandra Mack, MSW is the CVO of Strategies for Empowered Living Inc., a New York based human development company that offers workshops and products designed to help people succeed and grow. Cassandra is a trained social worker, nationally respected consultant and highly sought after speaker. She is the author 12 highly-successful books. Some of her popular titles include: "From The Block To The Boardroom: Power Tools for Black Men and The Women Who Love Them," "Smart Moves That Successful Youth Workers Make, and "The Single Mom's Little Book of Wisdom, "The Black Man's Little Book of ENCOURAGEMENT" For more information go to: www.strategiesforempoweredliving.com

What is the one thing that you would do if you knew you could not fail? Why haven't you done it already? Could it be that you are exerting too much energy thinking about what you do not have instead of taking stock of what you do have? Far too often, when people set out to do something new or difficult they focus on the skills and resources that they lack instead of looking at the things they bring to the table. They focus on previous attempts and past failures. They dwell on who's holding them back and who won't give them a break. Then, compile a laundry list of reasons why their plans won't work and their ideas won't fly. Before you know it, they talk themselves out of their dreams before they ever take the first step to get started.

This is one of the greatest acts of self-sabotage, because if you do not have the inner resolve to pursue your dreams, no matter what, you will never take the initiative to create the life you want. Believe it or not, nobody but you can hold you back. People can close a few doors. Make things harder. Refuse to share their resources. Unlevel the playing field. Change the rules midgame. They can even tell you that you will never make it. But they cannot stop your hustle. If you are to win the game of life, then you must develop the attitude that nothing will stand in your way. This means that when one door closes, you must find another. If you cannot find another, go through the basement or work your way up the ladder. If you cannot go through the basement, revise your strategy and try again. Then, wait until an opportunity presents itself. If an opportunity does not present itself, put your hustler's hat on and create your own. What great feats would you achieve if you wholeheartedly acted on your ideas? How might you change the world, revolutionize an industry and prosper your family and community?

It is important for you to know that every great movement, every great invention, every multi-million dollar company and every success story started out as an idea in somebody's mind. Michael Jordan's mastery of basketball started out as an idea in his mind. Tiger Wood's mastery of golf started out as an idea in his mind. Martin

Luther King's "I Have A Dream," speech started out as an idea in his mind. President Barack Obama's run for the presidency started out as an idea in his mind. Rap and hip-hop started out as an idea in someone's mind. What ideas do you have lying around in your mind that you need to act on quickly? Put your ideas on paper and act now. You cannot afford to sit around and complain that life is too hard and no one is willing to give you a break. If you do, life will pass you by and you'll go to your grave with your greatness still inside of you.

Action Steps

List one idea that you need to act on quickly, no matter how outrageous or farfetched it may seem. Write out the steps that you will take to act on this idea. Take one step this week.

In order to pump yourself up to act on your ideas quickly, talk to yourself as if you were training a heavyweight boxer for the fight of his life. Now bring that same fighter's spirit to the pursuit of your dreams.

CHILDREN CAN'T BE WHAT THEY DON'T SEE
By Sanya Hudson-Payne

Ms. Sanya Hudson-Payne was born and raised in Brooklyn, New York where she resides with her 17 year old daughter. She is the Vice President of 1209 Publishing, an author, radio and webshow host, radio producer, motivational speaker, educator and screenwriter who uses her brand as a vessel to encourage, empower and educate. In 2006 she became a published author with her well-received first novel, "The Seasons of Love" and her latest novel, "A Love I Can Trust" was released in early 2012. Ms. Hudson-Payne has a keen ability to empower not only youth but also professionals who are seeking to discover their Life's Purpose. In 2006 she was featured in Essence magazine as a successful businesswoman. She was asked to be the keynote speaker for the State of the Woman's Address in New York City, and hosted 1209 Enterprise's Pre-Affair with Susan L. Taylor. Using various venues to share her journey as a catalyst for change, she is a frequent guest on numerous radio shows and contributing writer for Sisterhood Agenda and City Path online magazines as well as the Associated Content Press. Ms. Hudson-Payne works with aspiring authors who have dreams of being published. In 2011, she executed her first successful Aspiring Writer's Short-Story Contest which garnered participation from writers as far away as Africa. Ms. Hudson-Payne is truly committed to advocating for the underserved and underrepresented. Her message to others, "No matter what stereotypes people are confronted with, my journey is a personal testament that roses can grow through concrete changing dilapidated shacks into mansions of splendor. Encourage, Empower and Educate!"

Cultivating greatness is an implicit responsibility we all have. My ancestors spoke of it and breathed it into my DNA; therefore, it is my duty to not only be great, but to nurture the sparks in others until it becomes an incandescent inferno. Mentoring youth is when I am at my authentic best; something happens to my spirit where it begins to sing a song of promise. My role as a mentor isn't solely to applaud a youth's strengths; it is to speak directly to their weaknesses. I implore my mentees to acknowledge their Achilles' heel as surmountable lies others have placed upon their shoulders. Once that happens, I provide my mentees with life experiences they will remember forever.

Recently, I began serving as a Community Advisory Board member of a charter school in New York. I intentionally accepted the charge to serve after reviewing data and confirming the student demographics' comprised of those stemming from low-income families. That was my story; a child who grew up in one of Brooklyn's housing projects and had to identify with the "By Any Means Necessary" mantra I often heard but didn't quite know how to execute. I wanted to be the voice of reason, the motivator of possibilities - the child of God who could make great things happen. At one board meeting, this question was posed, "Why is it difficult for black and brown kids to make it to college?" Everyone around me spoke of the financial hindrance families often encounter. I spoke of what I saw through my lens as a former educator in New York and Florida public schools, "Children Can't Be What They Don't See."

Transforming thought to action, I called seven of my college-age mentees in New York and told them, "Now it's your turn." They instinctively knew what I was alluding to and agreed to serve as mentors to students in the high schools where I serve on the board. To guarantee a well-crafted program, we held planning meetings to discuss program logistics. Some mentees, now turned mentors, traveled great distances to attend. The goal: Pass the baton to someone else. With 59 high school scholars signed-up, we were eager and prepared for the program's launch. My mentors don't know this, but I cried. I cried for God using me as a vessel to not change people, but to change their futures. I am alive and able to see my work transcend to another generation. I am able to smell my roses.

My program, Mentorship of Reciprocity, addresses two platforms: Personal Development and The College Process. When my mentors and I enter the school, the mentees run to us with infectious smiles on their faces geared up to learn and experience something new. To me, there is no greater joy than to add purpose behind a youth's heartbeat. For every word spoken, every lesson learned my message is to equip my mentors and mentees with the strength and courage to be uncompromising in their quest to be great. Ashe!

CLOSING REFLECTION

There is not a person that can truly say that he made it on his own. There was someone who poured into you; someone who opened a door for you; who taught you the ropes. Someone who saw promise in you before you may have seen it in yourself. You may not have called this person mentor but you certainly know that they showed up at a time in your life when you could not help yourself. Now it is your time to be that person in the life of a young boy or teen struggling to become a young man of promise or struggling to stay alive. Some would say that today's youth are more troubled than young people from past generations. What is closer to the truth is that while the beats, style of dress, hairstyles, sneakers, dating rituals all have changed; what never changes is self-destruction. It is still unapologetically fatal.

Our adversary has managed the feat of appearing to not exist. Our job is to expose the psyche master for what he is— a sneaky imposter who perfected the use of fear and doubt to pick off the young and the not-so-young. There you have it mentors, the expectation of a man called to minister as a mentor to young people that are expected to grow and take the place of their elders (us). Our job is to make beneficial deposits so that our mentees can make meaningful withdrawals that may save their lives.

My brothers, you have learned that mentoring is not just a program activity; it is not about getting your point across to young people; it is not about being loud, large and in charge; it is not about biding your time until a real ministry opportunity develops. Mentoring in a Christian context is about honoring a call from God to share your experiences, wisdom and love to another human being. It should also be clear that men need mentoring too and that only special men are prepared to mentor another man. While it was important to focus on developing young people, I hope and pray that the parallel goal of this book has been met and that is to make a huge life transforming gift deposit in your inner vault.

A pastor friend who mentors men and a mentee of mine started a ministry called Men on Fire. My prayer is that after completing this book, answering the questions, meditating on the reflections, raising questions and praying that you have indeed been transformed that you catch on fire and become Mentor Evangelists (Is this a new Ministry?). Like the Great Commission, you are tasked to go forth and spread the news that our young brothers need help. So share this book and what you have learned with other men. Hold sessions for men in your church with your pastor's approval. Take some of the sermons geared to young people and go over them with your mentees and teach and preach the contained truths to them.

The reality is that transformation will force you to see yourself, family, friends and institutions in a different light. Know that you move in power. Know that you can speak life to dry bones. I am excited by what God gave me to say in this book. The life experiences I have had; the ups and downs and the depression I suffered in my early 20's would all be used to liberate boys and men, most I will never meet. So go forth armed for the battle ahead and if you run across someone who challenges the merit or biblical mandate for your mentor ministry please offer the following:

> *Oh my people, hear my teaching; listen to the words of my mouth. I will open my mouth in parables, I will utter hidden things, things from old - what we have heard and known, what our fathers have told us. We will not hide them from their children, we will tell the next generation the praiseworthy deeds of the Lord, his power and the wonders he has done. Psalm 78: 1-4*

Peace...

AFTERWORD

Tribute For:
Pastor William Nathaniel Wyatt
January 29th 1921~ October 18th 2011

Honor your father and your mother, so that you may live long
Exodus 20:12a

During the writing of this book my beloved dad went home to be with the Lord. I was struck by the fact that here I was writing a book on mentoring and my dad spent most of his adult life being a "father to the fatherless." I expanded on the following article I wrote for a neighborhood newspaper about my dad. I thought that this should be the last Mentor's Reflection.

On October 19, 2011, I did something I never did in all of my 62 years on earth. I woke up without a father. My dad's Spirit left his pain-wracked body the day before. Over 1000 well-wishers filled First Baptist Church to witness and celebrate a Pastor's Homegoing. My dad, along with his wife Rev. Mae Wyatt, was co-founder and Pastor of Friendship Church of Christ Baptist. He served as Pastor for over 30 years. As his health began to decline he was elevated to Pastor Emeritus status.

William Nathaniel Wyatt, a tall, handsome, gentle and quiet strong man, was born in Bessemer, Alabama in 1921. He was the third oldest of 11 siblings born to Arthur and Pearl Wyatt. He married his childhood sweetheart and the one love of his life for 67 years Willie Mae Lewis. To this union William Curtis Wyatt, Lorraine Wyatt Puryear, Alfonso Wyatt and Deborah Leniece Wyatt were born.

Bubba, as he was affectionately called by his family, traveled North in the early 40's during the epic Great Migration. He joined millions of African-Americans riding the rails headed to places like: New York, Washington D.C., Chicago, Detroit and Los Angeles. He along with other sojourners looked to escape the racism of the South and find what was thought to be a better opportunity.

While the streets were not paved with gold my dad eked out a living to support his growing family. Over the course of his work life he held down as many as three jobs at one time to provide for his family. There were many nights that all he could do was make it home (It was my job to pick him up), grab dinner, have some Breyer's ice cream (known as The Leaf in our home) and fall asleep watching Perry Mason.

This I can say, he never failed to come home. He never 'lost' his paycheck or gambled it away. He never terrorized the mother of his children. He never ate the choice pieces of fried chicken first (he and my mom ate the back and wing). He was a strong, consistent, kind and loving presence. I must confess that we called our father 'electric chair' eyes while growing up. He could shoot a look that instantly killed all manner of foolishness.

My father was the father to many young boys and girls from the neighborhood who found their way to Friendship Church. One young man at my dad's Homegoing confessed to the audience during the Wake that he was a horrible, moody and mischievous child (was he ever!). He recounted the time when he was cutting class and bumped into Rev. Wyatt walking up the stairs during an unannounced school visit. That same young man, years later, graduated from college, was called to ministry and is a third year student at New York Theological Seminary.

None of Pastor Wyatt's biological children, not even his favorite 'lil' girl Deborah, had a problem sharing him with so many sons and daughters. After all, he was their pastor, mentor, father figure, friend and chief encourager. In his later years, he seldom raised his voice, and would exhibit a dry sense of humor that I discovered through my wife who always managed to sit next to him during family functions. He thoroughly enjoyed the raucous laughter that he was blessed to preside over. He could truly say, "It is well with my soul."

After several debilitating strokes, his home shifted to the ElmCare Center located several blocks away from his home and church. The staff and residents became extended family. Every Sunday, when dad was able, he would wait by the elevator to be picked up to go to church. He had to be the most well-dressed and clean shaven man in any facility in New York. After church the family would go to the local diner where he would have his favorite menu offering, lamb chop dinner. He would fake anger when I would take a big scoop of the ice cream the family's favorite waitress would bring to him. The table had shifted. The love and laughter followed.

When he could no longer journey out and it was clear (at least looking back) that he was slowing down, the family would visit him after church. To entertain him and help fight loneliness and depression, I started making up stories about Lil Nathaniel (his middle name) that mixed true elements of his life with creative fiction always punctuated by a mini sermon at the end. He being a good Baptist preacher would preach along with me much to the delight of the family and to himself. Like David, he encouraged himself. His power move would be to raise his arms like an archer, dramatically pause and then shout a robust GLORY!

One of the stories he loved was how Lil Nathaniel pitched a no-hitter for his college softball team (true story) and no one was there from either school to witness it. I ended that story with the divine assurance that while there were no people present, rest assured that the God of the universe got up earlyyy, earlyyyy, earlyyyyy and was sitting in the stands and saw the whole game. That would always make my dad smile his little boy smile which in turn would light up his wife and children. All would be well in that moment.

Lil Nathaniel was given a Valentine's Day basket that included a stuffed dog with an interesting 'smooshed' face. The dog, obviously hastily made, had a crooked eye and equally askew mouth. So now the stories about Lil Nathaniel included Ruffy the cross-eyed dog. Ruffy could always be found perched on my father's lap whenever he was in his wheel chair. We truly discovered the joy in simple things in those special moments.

I loved hanging out with him on Saturdays (he loved to watch Bonanza re-runs) when I was not working or away. After his first stroke we were both laying in his king-sized bed (that he made up every morning and all of his clothes were always in their place). Out of nowhere he said to me: "When I dream I see myself walking." I remember during one of our sharing sessions before his health failed asking for advice about preaching my first Father's Day sermon. My dad gave me this gift that he so richly shared with others throughout his life. He said, "Son any man can be a father but only a special man can ever be a daddy." We thank God that we were given a daddy. See you on the other side Lil Nathaniel. We love you...

MENTOR'S TESTIMONY
DOC!

By Casey Jones

Casey Jones grew up across the street from Pastor William Wyatt. Casey's mother joined Friendship Church of Christ Baptist, a small neighborhood church of families. Casey is a graduate of Rensselaer Polytechnic Institute. Upon graduation, he worked for Accenture, the world's largest consulting firm. He moved from a comfortable private sector job and went into teaching. He enrolled in The New York City Leadership Academy for aspiring school principals. He is currently the principal of a public high school for over age and under credited students. Casey is married to a teacher and has become a father (daddy) for the first time. His son's name is Xavier William Jones.

There is an urban legend that men when lost are afraid to ask for directions. Whether this is fact or fiction I believe we all have a desire to feel as if we are headed in the right direction and have control over our destiny. While my ability to travel from point A to B made me feel empowered growing up; my personal sense of direction (the person I wanted to be) made me feel like a mouse in a maze. Growing up in New York City there are many things that can destroy the potential of young people. Without a strong filter to read between the lines of temptation, young people consistently find themselves becoming an additional number to the overall statistics that define our generation.

I was blessed to have a mentor who was strategically placed in my life to help me develop my filter and create the capacity to make wise decisions that helped shaped the man who I am today; but also the father I wish to become. Reverend William Wyatt (aka Doc) was a blessed man that touched the lives of many young people. Being a pastor required him to support his congregation; in particular he had a strong focus on supporting young men without fathers. The young men that I grew up with and that I consider brothers all had a common thread; we had fathers who were not in our lives either by choice or by death. Boys without fathers feel abandoned and less than no matter how much support they may receive from their mother and others who care for them.

The relationship I was able to develop with my mentor allowed me the opportunity to have an escape from the daily challenges of being a young black man in America. In him, I developed a confidante with whom I was able to talk about many topics. His mentoring approach did not have office hours. He was available when needed and could always be counted on. Whether it was attending parent teacher conferences at school or taking you to a Mets game; his strategy was focused on engagement and encouragement.

His ability to support different types of people was amazing. When young men have emotional baggage, it manifests itself in a variety of ways. While I and the "boys" shared a common bond of lacking a biological father, we all expressed our frustration in different ways. Some of our anger showed up in school, in church, or even within our closest relationship(s) and with family members. Overall, I think the mentee/mentor relationship helped us overcome a myriad of issues we experienced as young men. As we matured we were able to channel these issues into productive behaviors.

I am comfortable with saying that his work with all his mentees instilled in us a belief that anything was possible if we had our priorities in place and were grounded spiritually. When you have a strong foundation of values you are able to navigate life in a manner that guides your decisions and provides you with consistency. As I reflect on my life, the late adolescence and early teen years were critical in my development and the four other young men I grew up with.

My mentor embraced me not only as an individual who could make decisions, but also as a son. As I continue to grow in my role as a mentor, I reference my experiences with "Doc" as a guide to help support the next generation as I was supported in the past. Even in his passing my mentor will continue to be one of the most important people in my life. RIP Doc!

SUGGESTED READING

A Leader's Guide to Real Men, Real Stories: Urban Teens Write About How to Be a Man, Youth Communication

All God's Children :The Bosket Family and the American Tradition of Violence, Fox Butterfield

A Hope in the Unseen: An American Odyssey from the Inner City to the Ivy League, Ron Suskind

America's Cradle to Prison Pipeline (A Report of the Children's Defense Fund), Washington: Children's Defense Fund, 2007

Building The Bridge As You Walk On It: A Guide for Leading Change, Robert E. Quinn

Celebration of Discipline: The Path To Spiritual Growth, Richard J. Foster

Changing' Your Game Plan: How to use incarceration as a stepping stone for success, Randy Kearse

Countering The Conspiracy To Destroy Black Boys, Jawanza Kunjufu

Dealing With Dad: Teens Write About Their Fathers, New York: Youth Communication

Emotional Intelligence, Daniel Goleman

Engaging the Soul of Youth Culture: Bridging Teen Worldviews And Christian Truth, Walt Mueller

Everything I'm Not Made Me Everything I Am: Discovering Your Personal Best, Jeff Johnson

Fist Stick Knife Gun, Geoffrey Canada

Flava of Youth Worship, The Living Pulpit, New York, 2003 Rev. Alfonso Wyatt

Growing Up Black: Teens Write About African-American Identity, New York: Youth Communication.

Help! I'm an Urban Youth Worker!, Ginger Sinsabaugh

How I Became An Angry Black Man: From Prison To The Pulpit, Rev. Darren Ferguson

Ignite the Fire: Kindling a Passion for Christ in Your Kids,

Barry St. Clair and Carol St. Clair

Khalil's Way, David Miller

Life Without Limits: Spiritual Growth for Teens,
Rev. James P. Quincy III

Manchild Dying in the Promised Land: Strategies to Save Black Males, Sallie M Cuffee.

May I Help You?: Seven Steps to Successful Youth Ministry,
Rev. James Quincy

Nurturing The Soul of the Youth Worker, Tim Smith

Reaching Up For Manhood, Geoffrey Canada

Revisiting Relational Youth Ministry: From a Strategy of Influence to a Theology of Incarnation, Andrew Root

Soul Be Free Poems Prose & Prayers, Alfonso Wyatt &
Ouida Wyatt

Souls in Transition: The Religious and Spiritual Lives of Emerging Adults, Christian Smith and Patricia Snell
Sparks: How Parents Can Help Ignite The Hidden Strengths

In Teenagers, Dr. Peter L. Benson

Starting Right: Thinking Theologically About Youth Ministry, Kenda Creasy Dean, and Dave Rahn

Tapping the Potential: Discovering Congregations' Role in Building Assets in Youth, Eugene C.Roehlkepartain and Glenn A. Seefeldt

The Black Male Handbook: A Blueprint for Life, Kevin Powell

The Black Man's Little Book of Encouragement, Cassandra Mack

The Community Church: Implementing the Gospel of Jesus, Rev. James P. Quincy III

The Gospel Remix: Reaching the Hip Hop Generation. Jamal-Harrison Bryant, William H. Curtis, Otis Moss III, Ralph C. Watkins, Jr.

The New Jim Crow: Mass Incarceration in the Age of Colorblindness, Michelle Alexander

The Pact, Sampson Davis M.D., George Jenkins M.D, Rameck Hunt M.D.

The Soul of Hip Hop: Rims, Timbs and a Cultural Theology, Daniel Hodge White

The Student Handbook To Breaking All The Rules, Alfred Blake

Toward a Prophetic Youth Ministry: Theory and Praxis in Urban Context, Dr. Fernando Arzola

Whatever It Takes: Geoffrey Canada's Quest to Change Harlem and America, Paul Tough

When The Tear Won't Fall: One Man's Journey Through The Intimate Struggles Of Manhood And Fatherhood, Kenneth Braswell

Who Moved My Cheese, Spenser Johnson

Who Will Speak for the Thugs?: The Promise of a Hip Hop Church, Eric Gutierrez

Unsigned Hype: A Novel, Booker T. Mattison

CONTRIBUTING WRITERS

CPSIA information can be obtained at www.ICGtesting.com
Printed in the USA
BVOW03s1351030314

346507BV00003B/15/P